Alan Ayckbourn

Twayne's English Authors Series

Kinley E. Roby, Editor
Northeastern University

TEAS 384

ALAN AYCKBOURN
(1939–   )
Photograph courtesy of Alec Russell

Alan Ayckbourn

By Sidney Howard White
University of Rhode Island

Twayne Publishers • Boston

Alan Ayckbourn

Sidney Howard White

Copyright © 1984 by G. K. Hall & Company
Published by Twayne Publishers
A Division of G. K. Hall & Company
All Rights Reserved
Published by Twayne Publishers
A Division of G. K. Hall & Company
70 Lincoln Street
Boston, Massachusetts 02111

Book Production by Elizabeth Todesco

Book Design by Barbara Anderson

Printed on permanent/durable acid-free
paper and bound in the United States of
America.

**Library of Congress Cataloging in
Publication Data**

White, Sidney Howard.
  Alan Ayckbourn.

  (Twayne's English authors series; TEAS 384)
  Bibliography p. 154
  Includes Index.
  1. Ayckbourn, Alan, 1939–
—Criticism and interpretation.
I. Title   II. Series.
PR6051.Y35Z95   1984   822'.914   84-8576
ISBN 0-8057-6870-X

To Paulie

Contents

About the Author

Sidney Howard White is professor of English at the University of Rhode Island. A New Englander by birth, he has lived for many years in Southern California, where he completed his undergraduate work at Loyola University and graduate work (M.A., Ph.D.) at the University of Southern California. At Loyola, he served as editor of the student newspaper for four years.

From 1953 to 1966, Dr. White was associate professor and head of the Department of English at Marymount College, Palos Verdes Estates, California. He has taught creative writing and literature at the University of California at Los Angeles Extension, and has been visiting professor of English at the University of Victoria, British Columbia. He has also published stories and poems, as well as having plays produced at the Marymount theater.

Dr. White returned to the East in 1966 to be director of English Studies in Extension for the University of Rhode Island, a post he held for five years. He now devotes himself to teaching and research, having published books on *The Scarlet Letter, The Great Gatsby,* and Arthur Miller. He is the author of *Sidney Howard* in Twayne's United States Authors Series. He regularly gives graduate seminars on Emerson, Hawthorne, Henry James, the 1920s, and dramatic literature.

Dr. White served with the U.S. Army in World War II in Okinawa in an antiaircraft radar unit. He is also a former president of the College English Association of Southern California and member of the Executive Board of the California Association of Teachers of English.

Preface

For seventeen years now theatergoers in Britain have grown accustomed to attending the annual Alan Ayckbourn contribution to national hilarity. True, the "hilarity" in time has deepened, but it is still good, exceptional theater. In one year, 1975, Ayckbourn had the outstanding record of five plays running at the same time in West End houses, a feat not seen since Noel Coward and Somerset Maugham fifty years earlier. The reason for the success lies in a number of directions. There is no doubt that his subject matter, the middle-class misadventures, is a guaranteed winner in a country which has long been the first to laugh at itself. There is something growingly familiar about the bumbling suitor, the up-and-coming merchant, the pompous leader, the martyr-mum, and even the compulsive kitchen cleaner.

The major source, however, for Ayckbourn's remarkable success must be the theater in Scarborough, where he is the director of productions. Two hundred miles north of London, in Yorkshire, the popular seaside resort is the spawning ground for all of the twenty-eight plays, most of which have gone on to the West End. With modest beginnings in the town library, the unique theater-in-the-round is now firmly established (in a converted school) as the cultural showpiece of the area, operating year round. For twenty-seven years, except for a five-year stint with the BBC, Ayckbourn and the theater have been synonymous. It is no longer unusual for the London critics to brave the North Sea storms in winter to review the latest Ayckbourn brainchild. What is even more remarkable is the fact that for fifty weeks out of the year, Ayckbourn is devoted entirely to direction and stage business until the time he steals away for two weeks or so to write the annual play. The entire process is a kind of weird psychological game:

Before he writes a play, he announces the dates when it will open at his theatre. Posters are printed, tickets sold, the cast hired. Then, three or four days before the opening rehearsal, he starts the play. All he has at this stage is a series of giant doodles, diagrams and strange shapes, like an abstract painting. He works through the night from 9 PM to 7 AM, sleeps until midafternoon, and slogs on. The night before the actors meet for the first rehearsal he runs off copies of the completed script and hurls them through the actors' letterboxes. The miracle is that he's never been late, never failed to produce.[1]

Ayckbourn readily admits that he wrote very quickly in order to get it over with—some plays take only six days. *The Norman Conquests* (1974), a trilogy, took eight. But then *The Norman Conquests* was something quite special. It may well have the most innovative structure in modern theater. Three over-lapping plays, each the offstage of the other, so that we, in a sense, follow the action when the characters move into another part of the house. However, one story alone is told in all three plays, and they can be seen individually or in any combination. The play was much admired, won a number of awards, moved on to New York, and probably firmly established Ayckbourn as a major force in contemporary theater.

The international reputation, ironically, was begun as early as the first successful production in London—*Relatively Speaking* (1967). This ingenious, little farce, openly modeled on every farce formula in the book, ran for a year, and was immediately followed by translations and productions throughout the world. It continues to find a ready audience wherever it is played. Even though Ayckbourn admits that "verbally his work is really extremely English in its tremendous understatement," he believes he has the explanation for the success of this and other plays outside of Britain. The plays often depend on the basic insecurities and gross inefficiencies of modern life. The condition is universal. "It starts," Ayckbourn says, "with the champagne bottle that refuses to break against the boat while they're playing the national anthem, and it goes right down to the scissors that won't cut, the lights that won't turn on. But the planet as a whole is increasingly urbanized. Everyone is trying to cope with a world that is increasingly mystifying, increasingly alarming." The net result, concludes Benedict Nightingale, is that "his plays raise suburban absurdities to the level of universal anxieties."[2]

There are enough suburban mishaps to keep Ayckbourn busy another fifteen years at least. The ones already explored are characteristically close domestic dilemmas. *Time and Time Again* (1972), a strong favorite with many, concerns the tribulations of Leonard, a kind of passive hero, cavorting in the house and garden of his sister's home. He also manages to "cavort" in the adjoining cricket field where he becomes an ignoble failure—although winning the girl he ultimately loses. With possibly the funniest act to be found in Ayckbourn, *Absurd Person Singular* (1973) presents a distressed, rejected matron trying to do herself in with as many ways imaginable, while party guests troop in and fail to recognize her otherworldly "aspirations." And, of course, *The Norman Conquests,* aside from the bold staging innovations, has the fascinating introduction of the guileless Norman ("I only want to make you happy") and the family he wishes to galvanize into daring joy.

Ayckbourn is also at his best in portraying women. The ability ranges from very theatrical emotional releases as evidenced with Diana in *Absent Friends* (1975) and Vera in *Just Between Ourselves* (1977) to the complete character studies of Ruth and Sarah in *The Norman Conquests.* Diana, for example, has a breathtaking scene toward the end of the play where all her anguish comes to a head and she recites a terrifying monologue of her youth and how all she really wanted was to join the Canadian Royal Mounted Police. The gradual deterioration of Vera is the substance of the entire play which finally culminates with her catatonic state at the end. Ayckbourn's ability in these bittersweet comedies in deftly confirming the comic and the serious is a high watermark in his skills as a mature comic dramatist. Certainly, what results has a sharper edge, and illustrates his own definition of comedy—tragedy that has been interrupted.

It is perhaps the fortunate size of *The Norman Conquests* trilogy that gives us the two exceptional character studies of Ruth and Sarah. We are able to see a number of sides of their complex selves, best summarized for now by noting that both women move from utter rejection of Norman at the beginning to complete capitulation by the end of the harrowing "journey." And this is far from a mechanical, farcelike contrivance; it all happens in clever demonstrations of believable human experience and understanding.

This study will attempt to introduce Ayckbourn and his plays in what is the first full-length investigation of his works. The method will be chronological, beginning with early trial works, and continuing through the seventeen London productions between 1967 and 1982. There is one new play every year except 1968 and 1971, and this is balanced by two in 1977 and three in 1980. A separate chapter will consider two musical productions—*Jeeves* (1975), a disappointing collaboration with Andrew Lloyd Webber, and the promising *Suburban Strains* (1980), a Stephen Sondheim kind of "study" of the modern woman. The last chapter will attempt to draw some connections between the plays, indicating the general development of the playwright from nimble worker of farces to a Chekhovian writer of comedy.

Sidney Howard White

University of Rhode Island

Acknowledgments

To Alan Ayckbourn, for his genial considerations and warm hospitality during my visit to the Scarborough theater. To Heather Stoney, for invaluable and timely assistance in a demanding transatlantic correspondence. To Margaret Ramsay Ltd., London, for generous access to her files as literary agent for Alan Ayckbourn. To *Times* Newspapers Ltd., London, for permission to quote from articles and reviews which appeared as follows: Irving Wardle, 30 March 1967, 6 August 1970, 9 August 1974, 7 April 1978, 19 January 1980; J. W. Lambert, 9 June 1974; Brian Connell, 5 May 1976; John Peter, 8 June 1980. To the *Observer*, London, for permission to quote from articles and reviews which appeared as follows: Robert Cushman, 8 July 1973, 20 March 1977; John Heilpern, "Striking Sparks off Suburbia," 13 February 1977; Janet Watts, 4 March 1979; anonymous review, 27 January 1980. To the *Daily Telegraph*, London, for permission to quote from articles and reviews which appeared as follows: Frank Marcus, 20 August 1972; John Barber, 5 July 1973, 5 June 1980, 15 October 1980; Robin Stringer, "Scarborough Fare," 5 April 1974. To Macdonald and Co., London, for permission to quote from Ian Watson, *Coversations with Ayckbourn* (1981). To Chatto and Windus Ltd., London, for permission to quote from Alan Ayckbourn, preface to *Joking Apart and Other Plays* (1979).

Chronology

1939   12 April, Alan Ayckbourn born in London (Hampstead), to Horace Ayckbourn and Irene Worley Ayckbourn. Father first violinist, London Symphony Orchestra; mother, journalist and novelist.

1952   Wins bank scholarship to Haileybury and Imperial Service College Herefordshire. Member of Senior Literary and Debating Society.

1956   Leaves Haileybury to join Sir Donald Wolfit's company at Edinburgh Festival as assistant stage manager.

1957   Summer, joins Studio Theatre Co., Scarborough, under Stephen Joseph, as a stage manager/actor.

1958   Writes first play, *The Square Cat,* under the name "Roland Allen." Opens at Scarborough in 1959.

1959   Marries Christine Roland, actress. *Love After All* (by "Roland Allen") opens at Scarborough.

1960   *Dad's Tale* (by "Roland Allen") opens at Scarborough.

1961   *Standing Room Only* (by "Roland Allen") opens at Scarborough.

1964   6 August, first London production of *Mr. Whatnot* opens at the Arts Theatre, for four weeks.

1965–1970   Drama producer, BBC Radio, Leeds.

1967   29 March, *Relatively Speaking* opens at the Duke of York's Theatre, London, for one year (originally titled *Meet My Father,* Scarborough, 1965). *The Sparrow* opens at Scarborough.

1969   9 April, "Countdown" (written 1959), one of an anthology of short plays by various playwrights, opens at the Comedy Theatre, London, for three months.

1970   Rejoins Studio Theatre Company (now Scarborough Theatre Trust Ltd), Scarborough, as artistic director of the Library Theatre. August, *The Story So Far* opens at Scarborough. 5 August, *How the Other Half Loves,* opens at the Lyric Theatre, London for two years (originally at Scarborough, 1969).

1971 29 March, *How the Other Half Loves,* first New York production. Runs three months.

1972 16 August, *Time and Time Again* opens at the Comedy Theatre, London, for seven months (Scarborough, 1971).

1973 4 July, *Absurd Person Singular* opens at the Criterion Theatre, London, transferring to the Vaudeville Theatre on 30 September 1974 for a total tun of two years, four months (Scarborough, 1972).

1974 1 August, *The Norman Conquests* opens at the Globe Theatre, London, for a year and a half (Scarborough, 1973).

1975 22 April, *Jeeves* opens at Her Majesty's Theatre, London, for one month. First musical collaboration, with Andrew Lloyd Webber doing the music. A failure. 23 July, *Absent Friends* opens at the Garrick Theatre, London, for nine months (Scarborough, 1974).

1976 Library Theatre moves to new premises, now Theatre-in-the-Round at Westwood, Scarborough. 19 May, *Confusions,* five one-act plays, opens at the Apollo Theatre, London, for eight months (Scarborough, 1974).

1977 16 March, *Bedroom Farce* opens at the National Theatre, London, transferring to the Prince of Wales Theatre on 7 November 1978 for a total run of two years, four months (Scarborough, 1975).

20 April, *Just Between Ourselves* opens at the Queen's Theatre, London, for five months (Scarborough, 1976).

1978 5 April, *Ten Times Table* opens at the Globe Theatre, London, for a year (Scarborough 1977). Summer, *Men on Women on Men,* musical revue with Paul Todd doing the music, opens at Scarborough (BBC-TV in 1979).

1979 10 January, *Sisterly Feelings* opens at Scarborough. 7 March, *Joking Apart* opens at the Globe Theatre, London, for four months (Scarborough, 1978). 28 September, *Taking Steps* opens at Scarborough.

1980 18 January, *Suburban Strains* (a musical play with music by Paul Todd) opens at Scarborough. 3–4 June, *Sisterly Feelings* opens at the National Theatre, London, for eight months. 2 September, *Taking Steps* opens at the Lyric Theatre, London for nine months (Scarborough, 1979). 25 September, *Season's Greetings* opens at Scarborough. 14–25 October, *Season's Greetings* opens at the Round House Theatre, London, for a limited run of ten days.

1981 5 February–14 March, *Suburban Strains* opens at the Round House Theatre, London, for a limited run of five weeks (Scarborough, 1980). Summer, *Me, Myself and I* (three musical shows with music by Paul Todd) opens at Scarborough. 2 October, *Way Upstream* opens at Scarborough. 16 December, *Making Tracks* (a musical play with music by Paul Todd) opens at Scarborough.

1982 24 February, *Way Upstream* opens at the Alley Theatre, Houston, the American premiere. 29 March, *Seasons' Greetings* opens at the Apollo Theatre, London. 3 June, *Intimate Exchanges* opens at Scarborough. 18 August, *Way Upstream* opens at the National Theatre, London.

Chapter One
The Life

Alan Ayckbourn was born on 12 April 1939, in London (Hampstead), the only child of Horace Ayckbourn and Irene Worley. The father, who died when Ayckbourn was very young, was first violinist with the London Symphony Orchestra. The marriage, however, had ended in divorce by the time young Ayckbourn was four; and the mother under the pen name of Mary James began a fairly successful career writing for women's magazines and doing novels. Ayckbourn recalls spending many hours as a child in the offices of women's magazines and in the women's press club. At home while mother typed away to earn their livelihood, Ayckbourn did his stint in some early writing.[1] Literature and theatricals both were family heritages: a maternal grandfather was a Shakespearean actor and manager, and his maternal grandmother (Lillian Morgan) was a male impersonator in English music halls. Both had long careers on the stage.

Life became more exciting for Ayckbourn when his mother married Cecil Pye in 1947. "Exciting" to the extent that it was to be a stormy ten-year marriage: "I was surrounded," Ayckbourn says, "by relationships that weren't altogether stable, the air was often blue, and things were sometimes flying across the kitchen."[2] Pye was a Barclay's bank manager and the family lived in a succession of flats above the banks in Sussex towns, Horsham, Uckfield, Billingshurst, Hayward's Heath, and Lewes. There were advantages of a sort, Ayckbourn recalls, in that he was a Cockney until the remarriage, and then "my accent got better."[3] These formative years, with their horrors and "compensations," became in time the setting for all his adult plays. Sussex suburbia with all its inherent absurdities was perfectly suited for successful theatrical "mining."

In 1952, Ayckbourn won a bank scholarship to Haileybury and Imperial Service College in Herefordshire, a public school. Barclay's Bank awarded three or four scholarships a year based on academic ability. After a loose and independent local boarding school, Haileybury was a shock, since it was run along traditional tight lines of authority. "Everything," Ayckbourn recalls, "was done to make you feel unwelcome."[4] In time Ayckbourn and the others developed a "defense" of their own and adopted a somewhat Bohemian manner. "We behaved as we thought artists and writers did . . . we didn't clean our studies much, and we were always a bit longer-haired than the others. We tended not to join in any of the functions, we were a bit anti-establishment, and we were thought of as a bit left."[5] The method seemed to work in that the masters left them more to themselves—and even left them out of responsibilities or student life advancements. If, as Ayckbourn recalls, he did lose out on the social side of things, he made up for it with a fair ability at cricket and rugby. There was also, of course, his interest in writing and the theater.

He wrote the house play which was presented at the end of each term. These were revue sketches. Ayckbourn was a member of the Senior Literary and Debating Society. He also edited the house magazine; and admits that because he was not too efficient as an editor, he always had problems getting contributions. It was not unusual for him to write them himself under various assumed names: "I used to type through the night on old stencils and the housemaster used to stand over me furious, because his house magazine was always later than everybody else's."[6]

Theater, more than anything else, soon became his chief school interest. Ayckbourn credits the French teacher, Edgar Matthews, a wild theater enthusiast, as the one who got him started in school plays. "There is always one master," Ayckbourn recalls, "who should have been in the theatre and happens to be school mastering instead, who spends his entire life avoiding the French syllabus and directing plays he wishes he'd directed elsewhere."[7] With Matthews leading the way, Ayckbourn soon found himself further and further away from the career of journalism he had had in mind. From the very start, the way of the theater was exciting and completely overwhelming. Matthews seemed to believe he had some talent as an actor and encouraged him in the school plays. The major goal was to be included in the annual Shakespeare tour out of the country during the school holidays.

Evidently, Matthews had gained considerable experience ("He was a wizard of organization") in what seems like a massive undertaking—shepherding teenagers around Europe and even to America. In the summer of 1955 they went "on the road" to Holland with a production of *Romeo and Juliet* in which Ayckbourn played Peter. The following summer they toured America and Canada with *Macbeth,* Ayckbourn playing Macduff. Such experiences were heady enough to convince young Ayckbourn that the theatrical life was the life for him, and to leave Haileybury behind. Matthews used his one major professional contact to secure a position for Ayckbourn as assistant stage manager (ASM) with Sir Donald Wolfit's Company at the 1956 Edinburgh Festival. The full theater life had, at last, begun.

Enter Actor

Ayckbourn fully admits that his willingness to work for a very low rate got him the job: "I played a sentry. Wolfit employed me because I'd been in the cadet force and could be guaranteed not to faint for forty minutes on parade. The last bloke had fainted on him in his big scene."[8] Watching the very theatrical Wolfit go through his mighty paces of loving and hating his audience was a course in theater life. Of course, simply being a part of this exciting new world was everything to the young Ayckbourn. He had the opportunity also to see a great deal of theater at the Festival. After Edinburgh he joined the Connaught Theatre Repertory Company in Worthing as an unpaid student/ASM doing a few bit parts. About this time he was beginning to believe that he was better suited for managing than acting. Nevertheless, during these early years he doggedly took on whatever parts he could get.

Ayckbourn's associations during 1957 managed to combine directing and acting: first, with Hazel Vincent Wallace's Repertory Company at Leatherhead as ASM and actor, and later with Frank Hauser's Repertory Company at Oxford. In the summer of 1957, prior to Oxford, Ayckbourn began his first association at Scarborough under Stephen Joseph as stage manager and actor. The fledgling theater was then called the Studio Theatre Company, and at the time Ayckbourn was not even sure where Scarborough was. Situated in Yorkshire on the East coast, a popular family resort, it seemed a good choice for the summer. The idea of theater-in-the-round also appealed to the practical Ayckbourn since there would be "no scenery to shift."[9] The choice was a fortunate one for both Ayckbourn and Scarborough since it was to be the beginning of a relationship which, now twenty-seven years later (and twenty-eight plays later), has made the names Ayckbourn and Scarborough synonymous. Five of these years, however, from 1965 to 1970, Ayckbourn tried his hand as a drama producer

at BBC Radio in Leeds. When he rejoined the company in 1970 it
was as artistic director, the man in charge.

Ayckbourn is the first to admit his complete debt to Stephen Joseph, who began a theater-in-the-round in Scarborough in 1955 in
the Concert Room of the town's public library. Joseph was a young
university lecturer, head of the drama department at Manchester
University, and the son of the veteran actress, Hermione Gingold.
Joseph's visits to America had inspired him to try this new kind of
theater in England. Thus the Scarborough Public Library became the
birth place of England's theater-in-the-round. Actually, Joseph's innovative company was a touring company much of the time with a
summer home in Scarborough. Supported by an Arts Council grant,
the company was encouraged to bring theater to the provinces.

Ayckbourn unreservedly considers Joseph to be his mentor in theater. In a time of conventional proscenium arch stages, Joseph was a
passionate extremist for his new kind of complete staging. Ayckbourn
holds the same view as Joseph that even the compromise stage, the
thrust stage, does not satisfy: "He believed that you should go the
full round or not at all." Nothing else would provide the sense of
theater that he believed in. According to Joseph, "the only thing that
mattered about theatre, when it came to it, was the actor and the
audience. This was the most important concept and the round, more
than any other medium, emphasizes this most strongly. The actor is
in the middle and the audience surrounds him and there's nothing
else, really."[10]

Economics may have been involved as well since large stages seem
to cry out for large and expensive sets. Joseph was able in his time to
prove the worth of productions that depended simply on the quality
of the essential play and less on fine trappings. Although Joseph saw
the writer and the director in secondary positions to the actors and
the audience, he nevertheless founded a kind of writer's theater at
Scarborough. David Campton, James Saunders, and Ayckbourn were
to be early "graduates." Joseph believed, as Ayckbourn does, that the
dramatist serves the actor: "Essentially the audience, whether they
like it or not, are watching the actor and not the dramatist. They're
watching the dramatist through the actor, and if you don't get your
actor right, there's very few dramatists who can actually survive."[11]

Joseph also stoutly believed that theater people should be *total*
theater people. Everyone should know what they could about the
other arts of the theater in addition to their own. In Ayckbourn's

case, the encouragement he was given by Joseph to do more with lighting and sound as well as acting is probably the basis for the early play successes. From the very start, then, Ayckbourn was able to use his wider stage interests in conceiving the written play. During these early years of theater apprenticeship, from 1956 on, Ayckbourn acted in a sufficient number of plays, both major and minor roles, to thoroughly understand the craft. He was Vladimir in *Waiting for Godot,* More in *A Man For All Seasons,* and Starbuck in *The Rainmaker,* to name a few. Together with his increasing competence as a stage manager and director, he was primed and ready for the new role of playwright which began in 1958 with Stephen Joseph's encouragement. "He had that ability," Ayckbourn recalls, "which one tries to retain in Scarborough, which is the ability to bring out talents people didn't know they had." It was also characteristic of Joseph that all the repertory players should be writing something or other. However, as Ayckbourn adds, "I think in his wisdom he saw that I wasn't going to make it as an actor, so it wasn't all that altruistic."[12]

"Roland Allen," Playwright

Using the name Roland Allen and being neither a singer nor a guitar player, Ayckbourn wrote his first play, *The Square Cat* (1958), about a pop singer, which part he of course played. Four other early plays were to follow under the same name. The pen name was derived from his wife-to-be, Christine Roland, an actress in the Scarborough Company. They were touring in a play called *Love and Chance,* and the publicity man suggested in Leicester that they become engaged as a press stunt. They went further than that and were married in 1959. The succeeding years as a husband and father of two and actor and struggling writer brought new demands that required novel solutions. It was at this time that Ayckbourn began his habit of writing late at night. He took on the chore of the night feeding ("all my early plays have got bottled milk all over them") and managed some sleep during the day.[13] In time the nocturnal writing habits became standard procedure, and he still writes all his plays in three or four all-night bouts.

Keeping the young family together at this time was not easy, and Ayckbourn recalls many trying moments into the early 1960s. At times they could only afford a tiny flat, and the eldest son slept in the bath tub. More early plays by "Roland Allen" followed. Each year a new one was produced at Scarborough. *Love After All* (1959) was advertised as "A gay, new farce, in Edwardian days, of love, folly and disguise." *Dad's Tale* (1960) is a Christmas show featuring a dance company, ideal for "adults and children alike." The last of the Roland Allen plays, *Standing Room Only* (1961), is an ingenious comedy with interesting overtones of the theater of the absurd. There are earnest attempts to bring it to the West End, but they never materialized.

Standing Room Only presents the ultimate traffic jam in London: the city is immobilized and everyone settles down—in bus or auto—to live their lives. The action of the play is a few hours in the lives of five characters living in a double-decker bus stuck on Shaftsbury Avenue. The driver sells his engine and starts a garden under the hood. John Russell Taylor admits "some slight sense of strain at spinning out one joke so far." However, Taylor does point to Ayckbourn's distinct gifts as a budding playwright, what in time will be his specialty—"the comedy of embarrassment with its characters trying desperately to continue living normal, respectable surburban lives in these very eccentric, public conditions."[14]

In the autumn of 1962 Stephen Joseph opened the first permanent home of his sometime traveling theater company at the Victoria Theatre, Stoke-on-Trent. Ayckbourn joined as actor/director and settled down for the next three years determined by now to overcome the economic straitjacket by some productive playwriting, this time under his own name. Putting aside *Xmas v. Mastermind* (1962) as an unimportant "first" attempt, Ayckbourn finally began to strike sparks with a curious play called *Mr. Whatnot,* which opened at Stoke-on-Trent in 1963. Unashamedly borrowing from everyone—from Ionesco to the Marx Brothers—and having three fourths of the play in mime, it nevertheless drew enough interest to warrant a West End production. Peter Bridge produced it at the Arts Theatre and it ran for four weeks in August 1964. The critics, however, were hard on it despite the fact that it evoked a great deal of laughter. J. W. Lambert complained that it was a "fearful waste of rehearsal time which must have been put into so much neatly executed mime."[15]

The effect on the young playwright, now a West End playwright, was devastating. He had serious doubts if he would ever write again. Ayckbourn chose to leave the Studio Theatre the following year, 1965, and took a position as a drama producer for BBC Radio in

Leeds. The massive BBC, what Ayckbourn calls "that great paternalistic womb for the wounded to crawl into," became more than a haven for the next five years. The experience was to prove immeasurably valuable for playwriting: "you learned to examine your craft because you had to explain to other writers submitting works what needed to be changed and why things didn't work."[16]

West End Success

Things *did* begin to work for Ayckbourn during these years. His first West End success, *Relatively Speaking,* opened in 1967 and ran for one year. Originally titled *Meet My Father,* it had been produced first at Scarborough in 1965. Critics were nearly unanimous in praising the return of good light farce to the London stage. Ayckbourn was hailed as the West End's answer to Broadway's Neil Simon, and a new Noel Coward. Ayckbourn readily admits that the play is a "fairly deliberately devised play" in the farce tradition; and that in the writing of it he was urged by Stephen Joseph not to hold back from writing a "well-made" play, "a play that in general terms is fairly actor-proof, well constructed and which works."[17] Success included a BBC television production as a "Play of the Month" and eventual translations into many languages. In Mexico the play was awarded a bronze plaque.

Another play, *The Sparrow,* opened at Scarborough the same year but went no farther. General opinion seemed to be that it was too much like *The Knack,* the Ann Jellicoe hit of 1961. Another chance at the West End presented itself in 1969 with the production of an anthology of short plays by various playwrights, entitled *Mixed Doubles,* which ran at the Comedy Theatre for three months." Ayckbourn's contribution was "Countdown," a slight thing about the "unspoken" thoughts of husband and wife, which he had written ten years earlier.

By 1970 he had regained enough confidence in his prospects as a playwright to give up the BBC post in Leeds and to return to Scarborough. There were changes: Stephen Joseph had died in 1966, David Campton succeeded him for awhile, and the Stoke Theater was now entirely separate from what was now called the Library Theatre of the Scarborough Theatre Trust, Ltd. Ayckbourn was now in complete charge as the artistic director. Of course during the years with the BBC, Ayckbourn had managed to remain very much a part of the

life of the Library Theatre. There was never any real doubt that the
Scarborough Theatre, with all its continuing problems of finance and
space, was the nourishing fiber of his theatrical existence. In 1969
and 1970 two more plays opened at the theater, one of which, *How
the Other Half Loves*, was to go on to the West End as a rousing
success.[18]

How the Other Half Loves opened on 5 August 1970 at the Lyric
Theatre and ran for two years, a remarkable accomplishment for the
young playwright. The novel idea of running two stories, two different homes, on one set came about as a practicality since the open
stage at Scarborough was always representing multiple places. In addition, Ayckbourn frankly admitted that for the first time he was "a
bit exhausted" at the prospect of writing the usual annual play, so he
thought "I'll try writing two at once. Let's be clever."[19] The result
was great comedy and a starring vehicle for Robert Morley. The following year, 1971, the play became Ayckbourn's first New York production, running for three months with Sandy Dennis and Phil
Silvers.

The year 1971 continued to be a productive one for Ayckbourn: a
children's one-act play, *Ernie's Incredible Illucinations*, opened in London; and *Time and Time Again* opened in Scarborough and went on to
London in 1972. The play ran well for seven months and clearly
marked an advance in Ayckbourn's handling of light comedy. It was
an experiment, Ayckbourn acknowledged, "in which I wrote about a
totally inert central figure."[20] The result was a kind of "comic Hamlet of the cheaper suburbs" which the press and the public warmly
welcomed.[21]

The conquest of the West End continued in 1973 and 1974 with
two more major productions: *Absurd Person Singular* (1973) and *The
Norman Conquests* (1974). With these two successes there was no
doubt that a new Noel Coward had taken a strong hold of West End
theaters. *Absurd Person Singular*, playing successively at two theaters,
ran a total of two years and four months. *The Norman Conquests* ran a
year and a half at the Globe Theatre. The awards began to accumu-
late. Both plays won the *London Evening Standard* Drama Award as
the best plays of their year. *Plays and Players* chose *The Norman Conquests* as the Best Play of 1974, and the Variety Club of Great Britain
named Ayckbourn the Playwright of the Year.

Absurd Person Singular went on to a spectacular success in New
York in 1974, running for two years and being named as Broadway's

longest running current production. To mark the occasion, in 1976 the street sign at Broadway and 45th Street was changed to "Ayckbourn Alley." The success was even more enjoyable to Ayckbourn since he had wisely resisted a request from the New York producers to interchange the last two acts and leave the audience with more uproarious laughter. The play told the story of three successive Christmases, with all the action presented in three different kitchens. However, the structural novelties in *The Norman Conquests* surpassed everything Ayckbourn had ever tried before. The play was actually a trilogy with three plays being presented on alternate evenings—and the clever trick was to have each be the offstage of the others, showing what transpired when the same characters went into another part of the house. All three plays, in effect, told the same basic story.

In the winter of 1975, the Library Theatre expanded its productions into a nine-month season. Despite the increased demands on Ayckbourn—demands, of course, which he warmly welcomed—he still managed to open two new plays in London. The greatest challenge of all was *Jeeves,* his first musical collaboration with Andrew Lloyd Webber of *Jesus Christ Superstar* fame. Notwithstanding the enormous efforts, which grew to include the lyrics as well as the book, the production was a failure, lasting only one month. The large number of people involved and the general inexperience of the company ("We badly needed Hal Prince, or someone like him") made it a frustrating disaster.[22] Nevertheless, the experience of working with a musician gave Ayckbourn the confidence that something better along these lines could come in the future.

The other play of 1975, *Absent Friends,* had a mixed reception. Concerned about death, it confused the critics who had expected another farcical comedy. Ayckbourn saw the play as a definite advance in his abilities: "I was trying to do something much more low-key. It seemed to me that, if I was going to progress as a dramatist, I must try and get more comedy from character and less from artifically induced situations."[23] Writing the play at a different time of the year than usual, Ayckbourn called it the beginning of his "winter plays."

Another major "new beginning" came in 1976 when the theater moved to a temporary home of their own—their first after twenty-one years—to Westwood, a converted Victorian school. It was a hard won, stopgap refuge until their own theater is constructed. Leaving the concert room of the town's library behind, they could now plan on a nearly full year of stage productions. The theater had come a long way under Ayckbourn's direction. He proved to be an excellent administrator as well as an idea man. With Ayckbourn the company became an integral part of Scarborough by providing children's shows and community projects and by making the rounds of pubs and local halls. They had advanced far beyond their initial modest role as a summer tourist attraction. The truth, however, remains that with Ayckbourn's growing international prominence as a playwright, the company is becoming good business for Scarborough. It is no longer unusual for London critics to journey to Scarborough in the dead of winter to preview next season's West End productions.

The National Theatre

Confusions, a group of five one-act plays, played in London for eight months in 1976. The following year brought another notable comedy, *Bedroom Farce,* to London, this time to the National Theatre under Peter Hall's direction. After nearly two and a half years in London (including a transfer to another theater), the play arrived in New York in 1979 to great acclaim. It was one of the few times a British company was allowed intact on Broadway. The year 1977 saw another Ayckbourn London opening, *Just Between Ourselves,* which won the *London Evening Standard* award for Best Play of the Year.

The annual invasion of the West End continued with *Ten Times Table* in 1978 for a year's run and *Joking Apart* in 1979 for four months. *Ten Times Table* continues the out and out comic vein, this time about a small town festival committee planning a pageant. *Joking Apart,* in contrast, adds some sober Chekhovian considerations of suburban life, "enough to make this comedy of uncomfortable home truths grate even while we laugh at it"—so wrote Eric Shorter in the *Telegraph,* and other critics seemed generally to agree.[24]

The year 1980 was a banner one for London productions with three playing at one time. In June the much talked about *Sisterly Feelings* opened at the National Theatre, this being actually two plays since there are alternate middle acts. Ayckbourn's well-known wizardry hit a new zenith with a changeable structure which rests on a toss of a coin by two sisters to see who gets a coveted male. Depending on which night you attend, you see either the "Dorcas" play or the "Abigail" play. *Taking Steps* provides another novelty since much of the action revolves literally about the ascending and descending of imaginary stairs. This play starred the popular and beautiful television star Nicola Pagett. *Punch* called it the "Best farce in town." The arrival of *Season's Greetings* in October 1980 to the Round House Theatre for a limited run was another special event. For the first time London would have a chance to see what Scarborough audiences had delighted in for years—an Ayckbourn play done by his own company and also in the round. "The joy of this," John Barber writes, "is a simple but considerable one. Ayckbourn writes 'company' plays. He needs no stars. If one outstanding personality dominates the cast, some of the delicate balance is lost."[25] Balancing *is* required since this is another sardonic as well as hilarious look at a suburban Christmas gathering.

The disastrous *Jeeves* experience of 1975 had not been entirely wasted on Ayckbourn. At the time he felt that the close working relationship with the talented Andrew Lloyd Webber "might lead to something else, something conducted on our own terms." At the same time he was also attracted to a production like Stephen Sondheim's *Company* (1970), a clever musical rendition of city life. "A commuter-belt musical with an original book" might well suit an English audience.[26] Early in 1981, Ayckbourn mounted a major musical collaboration, this time with Paul Todd of the company. *Suburban Strains* moved Ayckbourn a number of steps closer within the challenge of a complete musical theater. In many ways this production is the further development, also with Paul Todd, of a musical revue, *Men on Women on Men,* which Ayckbourn ran as a late-night show during the 1978 Scarborough summer season. It was also run on BBC television.

Suburban Strains, with eighteen integrated musical numbers, is a swift-moving account of the emotional fortunes of Caroline and was generally greeted as a success. There was the further advantage of having the Scarborough company again appearing at the Round House Theatre. Ayckbourn continued at Scarborough with two more musical collaborations with Paul Todd in 1981—*Me, Myself and I* and *Making Tracks. Me, Myself and I* presents three interlinked musical shows, three aspects of the same woman. For the Christmas season, Ayckbourn wrote *Making Tracks,* a show business kind of entertainment set in a recording studio.

However, the major accomplishment for 1981 seems to be *Way Upstream,* in which Ayckbourn floods the stage to float a real, working boat. The Scarborough program describes "a tale of mutiny and piracy aboard a cabin cruiser on a sleepy English river." According to Anthony Curtis, the play (and the boat) moves through nautical farce into out and out fantasy, ending up in a "kind of up-dated adult version of *Peter Pan*." However, the maneuverability of the vessel undeniably holds the chief attraction. Curtis points to "the ingenuity of the stage-staff who arrange for it to glide under bridges with an echo-effect, pause at locks, weigh anchor in the moonlight, and tie up beside a private island with its own little wooden jetty."[11] It may well be," Curtis concludes, speaking of Ayckbourn's twenty-sixth play, "the most daring thing he has done."[27] The American premiere of this work took place 24 February 1982, at the Alley Theater in Houston.

Play Without End

For summer production at Scarborough, opening 3 June 1982, Ayckbourn has put together what may be his most daring theatrical innovation—*Intimate Exchanges,* eight plays in one. Granting that it all may be theatrical tight-rope walking, Ayckbourn has gone even further than the multiple scene options in *Sisterly Feelings* to dramatize the issue of chance in our lives. The play starts with a woman choosing or not choosing to have that first cigarette of the day. Whichever her choice, various play "options" will then open up into a series of "chanceful" possibilities.

The program bravely explains, "The two quite separate chains of events that result from her choice lead, by the end of scene one, to another character making two further decisions, this time of a slightly more important nature. Just before the interval two more choices, more crucial still, are to be made. Finally, preceding the fourth and final scene, another two major courses of action remain to be chosen by the characters." The results provide an opportunity for the audience to see one strand "of a much larger web of interconnecting alternative scenes." The apparent aim is to rouse the curiosity of the audience to return later nights and see other possibilities.

The program provides a double-page chart of "where *Intimate Exchanges* can lead you," looking very much like a molecular structure "road map." For example (following the chart), if the woman with the cigarette goes one way, a gardener will call five seconds later, and in five days the woman will be either into a scene called "a gardener in love" or into a scene called "the self-improving woman"—and then further and further as chance develops. If she had gone the other way with the cigarette choice, then five seconds later a friend would visit; and five days later either of these two scenes would be played—"dinner on the patio" or "confessions in a garden shed"—and, again, further and further chance developments five years later.

To simplify things somewhat, all the parts in all the versions are played by two actors, Lavinia Bertram and Robin Herford. Knowing full well Ayckbourn's fascination with challenging stage demands—in set design and acting—it comes as no great surprise that he would take on a summer project of this complexity. Two weeks after the opening, the company was still slowly introducing more versions into the repertoire. Ayckbourn's closing remarks in the program hint rather broadly at the nature of these "private" amusements: "How fast the whole project comes together will depend on the reserves of stamina of all of us—in particular the brave and remarkable cast of two whom I particularly wish to thank for agreeing to take part in this piece of theatrical lunacy."

Ayckbourn Today

The Alan Ayckbourn you meet today is an unprepossessing figure for the kind of success and acclaim he has received. A tall, rather roundish form with an open, friendly, country face—altogether far more in harmony with his Yorkshire neighbors than the Sussex towns he grew up in and writes about. Robin Stringer describes him well: "He talks fast and restlessly. His eyes dart occasional penetrative looks, as if testing audience reaction, from beneath an enormous forehead which, made higher by a receding hairline, slants down to an impressive overhang. He walks as he talks with a sort of eager, loose-limbed gait. It is as if the public schoolboy who left school at 17 to join the theatre and the underfed, underpaid actor of those early years have not quite come to terms with the well-fed playwright of the present."[28]

Ayckbourn lives in what used to be a vicarage, a modest house which sits high on the hill overlooking the Scarborough seafront. The house was once the home of his predecessor, Stephen Joseph. The small rooms are filled with hi-fi equipment, recorders, and games that he is fond of. Although he does not play a musical instrument, music matters a great deal to him. Puzzles of all kinds have always fascinated him. Critics have long pointed out that his plays are like Chinese boxes. The theater that is his whole life is only a few miles away, now established in a converted school building. The question continually put to Ayckbourn concerns his long residence in Scarborough, since he now has the means to live almost anywhere. And in the same light, one wonders why he has not joined other successful Britishers in the fashionable role of the tax-expatriate?

Such speculations always make Ayckbourn smile, for they overlook the fact that he is fundamentally a stage man, someone who runs an active, year-round theater, and that the playwriting which has given him fame is only a small part of his life. Moreover, Scarborough is his "grass roots"; he is, by admission, a great eavesdropper. And the town, with the summer tourist or without, is a mine for the kind of material he needs. "Scarborough is the sort of town," Ayckbourn explains, "where one couldn't live at jet set level even if you wanted to. The easiest way to get about is walking or busing. There's no car parking, so I am almost compelled . . . to live like an ordinary resident, which means that I spend all my time overhearing by accident."[29]

The amount of time during the year that Ayckbourn spends writing plays is incredibly brief. Some time around November, he slips away into an all-night routine for about a week and emerges eventually with a new play for the Christmas season. He writes very quickly; most plays take only six days—*The Norman Conquests,* trilogy and all, took eight. By now, the actual process is a proven, successful pattern: "I write out a script in long hand, which is a sort of a master plan of all the scenes and construction and then I start dictating. Often things get hopelessly out of hand. Speeches take off, characters take off and they are a series of improvisations. It's quite interesting to work that way. At least everything I've said is spoken once, even if it's only by me and if I can say it, then an actor can say it." The dictation is always done to Heather Stoney, Ayckbourn's longtime companion, who is also an actress. "If she laughs," Ayckbourn continues, "we're all right. I need the sound of my own voice in my ear to do this. It gives me a shape on a character's speech patterns, because I can mimic."[30]

Ayckbourn is also quick to admit that writing is an exhilarating experience for him—once he gets down to it. As soon as he has finished one play, he often feels anxious to go on immediately to another one. True, the euphoria might be misleading since he knows what difficult work the entire process really is. Moreover, he also knows he must turn away from the desk and back to running the theater. Nevertheless, he wisely finds the time to make a few notes, sketch out a few ideas for the next play. Of course, when play writing time comes (around nine months later), many of these "wonderful ideas" may not work, but often he has written "the idea that's been behind them." The process is a kind of now slow, now fast accumulation:

Things keep happening. Things add to an idea. It feels like a stone and it rolls; and little things stick on it. I need about eight ideas—well, not quite eight, but I need several—to make a play. I'm not happy when I just have an idea about a wife leaving a man and him inviting another bloke in to read the letter. I need two more, like the bedrooms, and the man who drives everyone to sleep; and when I've got those three going together, then I think: "Now we'll be able to get something to happen. Now the chemistry is flowing for a play, as opposed to a sketch."[31]

The well-working process has continued now for twenty-three years and twenty-eight plays. The center of his life, nevertheless, is still the Scarborough theater itself and the total responsibilities which go far beyond writing plays. Perhaps, it is this centering on production and its day-to-day demands that has made him the successful playwright he is. He seems fully content with his life and has no intention of moving on or trying other fields. If that time should ever come, Ayckbourn firmly believes that his successor should be someone of equally strong identity. If not, "they should close the place and say: 'You've had your theatre, Scarborough, and that's it.' And the Arts Council should bundle up their grant and look around for someone else they fancy. And it should always be a person or, better still, a group of people. It shouldn't be a building."[32]

Chapter Two

The Early Work

It is not unusual that the first attempt at play writing turns out to be a starring vehicle for one ambitious actor. The actor, naturally, is the playwright himself in a wild romp of a play, *The Square Cat* (1958), in which he plays a guitar player and a pop singer, talents which, quite perversely, Ayckbourn did not possess. The advertisement read: "A pop singer (with a difference) at loose in a very steady (supposed to be) household."[1] Very little need be said of the two others which followed, *Love After All* (1959) and *Dad's Tale* (1969)— both fledgling attempts for the actor/playwright. The first is a conventionally plotted farce, set in Edwardian days, of the mean father attempting to marry off the beautiful daughter to the rich suitor. Somehow, true love wins out in the end. *Dad's Tale,* a Christmas show, is a light entertainment that used the British Dance Drama Theatre.

Ayckbourn's real talents as a writer began to show themselves in the very clever *Standing Room Only* (1961). He postulates a London of the future in which a tremendous traffic jam brings everything to a halt. The premise opens up a number of good comedy possibilities which Ayckbourn handles with ingenuity and imagination. Londoners are immobilized where the jam leaves them; people camp out in cars and buses throughout the West End. The plot focuses on one family living for years in a double-decker bus. The bus driver believes—in the long stretch of time—that "the destination board on his bus is announcing his own surname—with the letters BRDWY after it standing for 'Best Ruddy Driver We've 'Ad Yet.' "[2]

Mr. Whatnot (1964), Ayckbourn's first London production, was fair game for the critics.[3] It must frankly be admitted that the notion of having so much of the play in mime is a bit bold. "You can't use the style of Marcel Marceau," Eric Rhode pointed out, "and expect your actors to create a story out of nothing."[4] Nevertheless, Ayckbourn does work out a rather involved, sometimes interesting, complete plot. The hero, Mint, a mute piano tuner, is let loose on a stately home, falls in love with the Lord's daughter, and in a series of farcical set pieces manages to win her. Basically, this is nearly identical to the first two plays of the "Roland Allen" era. It would seem that the idea is obsessive in Ayckbourn to have some outsider/hero run wild through a proper setting. Strong traces of Chaplin and the Marx Brothers are clearly evident: the movement is at a clockwork pace, often completely abstract yet humanely pathetic, interesting, and always hilarious. There is never any doubt that a complete knowledge of stagecraft on the part of Ayckbourn makes everything click.

Some of the movements in and out of reality are accomplished with clever sound effects. For example, the male gathering talks animatedly of their World War II battle experiences. The talk comes faster and faster and eventually we hear the sound of shells landing. All hide on one side of the table and lob food as grenades. Finally, Mint waves a white handkerchief, which is dismissed at first—and then accepted when he "throws a grenade" and wins the victory. Military salutes follow quickly, all are pleased, our hero kisses Amanda, the daughter of the house, and Lord Slingsby-Craddock, her father, shows Mint to his room for the night. End of act.

Carefully orchestrated movements support the best comic scenes. At a big meal-table scene, for example, Mint drinks too much and slides below the table. While the diners above the table become politely mystified by disappearing glasses and plates, Mint proceeds under the table to eat his way around. Other similar devices move the play along and make it a sufficiently comic entertainment despite obvious structural weaknesses, which the critics were quick to point out. According to Rhode, the second half is "mostly padding" and a "poverty of dialogue"; nevertheless, he admits that the audience "were collapsing in laughter."[5] However, there was not enough to sustain the production beyond four weeks.

The Sparrow (1967) concerns the misadventures of Ed, a mild-mannered bus conductor, and his roommate Tony, a car salesman with grand ideas for self-advancement. Ed brings Evie home one night, as sanctuary from a fierce rain storm. They had met at the dance hall. She is persuaded to spend the night because of the bad weather, but chooses the bathroom rather than the bedroom after she realizes what the enterprising Tony has in mind. Things become a bit complicated at this juncture in the plot. It seems that Tony, who pretends to be a businessman, plans to take the gullible Evie on as his secretary. In addition, we learn that there is an estranged wife of Tony's, Julia, who is still a road block to her husband's further social (and "business") designs.

In time, Evie learns the truth of Tony's deceptions which had been diverting her on-again off-again affair with the persistent Ed. It is now apparent that Tony had been using her to get even with Julia and with Ed (who had once been Julia's lover). The play ends with a big fight between Tony and Julia, a not entirely unwelcome sign that they were back together again. Quick to learn, Ed and Evie head for the nearest pub, vowing never to marry.

The Story So Far (1970)

Looking back, Ayckbourn readily admits that *The Story So Far*[6] is "probably not vintage, but it's got a few good laughs in it."[7] Revised a number of times, the play probably has too much of everything in it. However, it is worth some review here to see how the rather fantastic conception heralds a better play to come, *Sisterly Feelings,* ten years later. Characteristic of Ayckbourn, he is attracted to the stage possibilities of alternate choice, the way chance or accident affects our lives. The theatrical trick is to find some way of staging the *other* as well as the actual lives. Here we have the situation of three daughters and their husbands; and, as Ayckbourn has worked it out, "In each the daughter has a different husband, and they change around; the premise of the play being that, depending on who you marry, you become slightly different."[8]

Edward and Emma Gray are the parents of three sisters, Polly, Jenny, and Deirdre. In the first scene, we have Jenny (many children and pregnant again) married to Oliver; Polly married to David (bespectacled, frenzied, and fussy); and Deirdre dating James (a "lost young man"). In their living room, replete in middle-class comfort, the parents are celebrating their thirty-second wedding anniversary. Edward admits to Emma that he has doubts about some of the choices their daughters have made. He strongly believes that most people chose the wrong spouse—except themselves. However, we hear in the conversation of the children that the parents are a bit strange. Deirdre tells her guest, James, that "I barely like them," and needs his support when at home. In the course of the afternoon, both married couples express outright dissatisfaction with their marriages.

Credulity begins to stretch a bit when we have the evidence of the parents' strange ways. Rather abruptly, absurdities enter the play without the careful preparation they require. (Out and out farce, of course, would need none.) Jenny announces tea to father and he throws a book at her. Polly reveals the dark secret that "father is trying to kill mother." It seems that a snoopy neighbor had seen Emma gasping for breath in the greenhouse with father apparently unconcerned—and had written to the daughter. What are they to do? Jenny suggests that he is probably upstairs building a bomb. There is more effective humor in the ruckus caused by James and Deirdre presenting flowers to Emma. Deirdre is assailed by the others for being stupid; they had picked Dad's flowers and "he counts them."

The second scene presents the same situation, a few seconds later, but with the marriages changed around—the "other" chance that Ayckbourn is experimenting with. Now, Deirdre is married to Oliver, Jenny to David, and Polly has James (again) as the guest. We learn of additional disadvantages in the new combinations: money matters, children problems, and so forth. "When Oliver and I decide on a family," Deirdre says, "the first thing I shall get is an *au pair*." Oliver snaps back, "prefer that to a child, I must say." The scene ends with weak attempts to characterize the odd nature of the father, and resigned comments from Emma that "it makes no difference who you marry, you get what you deserve!"

In the third scene, partners change again: Polly now with Oliver, Deirdre with David, and Jenny with James. However, again, their differences and problems simply increase. A series of crazy events— suspected poison drink for father, a stepladder fall, hacksaws being brandished, someone collapses—lead us wearily to the final and strangest scene of all.

Here, Ayckbourn brings on *all* the possible couples—eighteen players in all—wearing names and numbers ("Deirdre 1," "Oliver 2," "James 2"). It is difficult to say what is accomplished with such a full stage. Their marital complaints simply continue. More strange events follow. The play ends with Edward and Emma going off for a walk and the children calling after them, concerned for their safety.

Chapter Three
Musicals

Jeeves (1975)

From its very first conception, Ayckbourn's first musical production, *Jeeves,* could be called nothing less than "momentous."[1] All the elements for a major theater piece were present. Drawn from the master comic writer, P. G. Wodehouse, and his popular stories, with music by Andrew Lloyd Webber and lyrics by Tim Rice (collaborators in *Jesus Christ Superstar*), book by Ayckbourn, and under the direction of the current master of comic direction, Eric Thompson, how could anything go wrong? But evidently it did, since it ran for a disappointing one month and was widely labeled a failure.

Jeeves became "a bigger commitment than I had originally envisaged," Ayckbourn told Michael Coveney. It turned out that Tim Rice "couldn't cope with the lyrics, so I got conned into doing them—as well as the book."[2]

However, some initial encouragement followed from the author when Webber and Ayckbourn "took their songs and lyrics to Wodehouse's Long Island home. Webber rehearsed some at the piano. To their relief, the master approved."[3] The idea of a collaboration with a musician proved stimulating to Ayckbourn, and the book quickly grew to an overlong four hours. And here was where the actual problems became apparent. Left to his own usual, independent devices at Scarborough, Ayckbourn could have "cut it in about a day." But this proved impossible in a production where musicians and actors already had their favorite number and parts: "it was like treading on eggs." The new discordant "elements" needed a strong unifying hand. "The producer of *Jeeves* [Bob Swash]," Ayckbourn relates, "I met twice as he spent most of his time in Los Angeles. We were all left to our own devices, which would have been all right if any of us had done this sort of show before. We badly needed Hal Prince, or someone like him."[4]

Jeeves is based primarily on Wodehouse's *The Code of the Woosters* (1938). Following the author's well-known interest and parodies of 1920s musical comedy, Ayckbourn appropriately makes *Jeeves* into a musical comedy narrated by our hero, Bertie Wooster. (Wodehouse thought of his novels as musical comedies without music.)

What we have here, in effect, is a mocking version of the form, somewhat like the very successful *The Boy Friend* (1954). The set, then, requires a stage within a stage, and we are witness to a performance being put on at the "East London Club for Unmanageable Boys." Having Bertie as both narrator and participant works very well in bringing out the humorous characteristics of the principals. Such devastating sketches are, of course, Wodehouse's stock in trade. For example, Bertie describes the villain of the piece, Sir Roderick Spode, "as a man who looks as if Nature had set out to make a gorilla and changed his mind at the last moment."

The plot is deliberately an old-fashioned farce: everyone is in love with someone else who is in love with someone else. Sir Roderick Spode and shy Gussie Fink-Nottle are rivals in the pursuit of Madeline Bassett, who wants a renewal of her love with Bertie, which once flourished on the Riviera. Bertie, as narrator, comments on the portentous size of Spode in pressing his suit—"Gussie's rival for Madeline's hand. Although from the look of Spode it didn't look as though he'd settle for less than an arm." Bertie's task, in dress suit and monocle, is to keep the show going with interspersed wit and musical entertainment. He plays his banjo, sings his lyrics, and is joined at times by a very clever excuse for a chorus line, what Ronald Bryden calls "a hand-picked all-male spectrum of vacuous bachelordom from the Drones Club, stepping with amateur zest, high, wide and all over each other's feet."[5]

Ayckbourn's lyrics are well matched to Wodehouse's unique style and substance, particularly the clever fractured quotations and overworked clichés. Bertie sings the song, "Travel Hopefully."

> As Nelson said at the battle of Waterloo
> 'Tis a far better thing I've done than I ever do
>
> For there comes an affair in the tides of men
> When that moment of truth that crops up now and then
>
> Requires a man to muster all his powers
> And set his face to meet his Totleigh Towers

I've invariably found
That feet kept on the ground
Allow the grass to grow

"Chok'd with ambition." At all times, in Bertie's dual roles, Jeeves, his loyal valet, is by his side offering help and even correction for the accounts of the wild escapades. At times, Bertie protests the need for such accuracy "in the broad sweep of things"; but, nevertheless, "to satisfy you" he goes back over the details. The result is a furthering statement which makes things even more complicated. In exasperation, Bertie warns his "guide": "There is accuracy and accuracy, Jeeves. You must learn the difference." On the other hand, Bertie has some marvelous comic misquotations of Jeeves:

BERTIE.   What's that bit you normally say about being smoked with
          the elastic of the cleaner shorts, Jeeves?

JEEVES.   Chok'd with ambition of the meaner sort, sir.

The net effect is to provide excellent parodies of village-hall theatricals. In the meantime, the curlicued plot goes forward. Bertie offers to help Gussie woo Madeline, and part of the key to success lies in finding Gussie's long-lost notebook. Bertie sings of "Wooster's Rescue Service."

Another part of the plot involves Stiffy Byng's love for Harold "Stinker" Pinker, the muscular clergyman. She wants to pretend marriage to Bertie so that her uncle will approve the man she really wants—Pinker. When Bertie protests, Stiffy warns him that she "could make things awfully hot for you. . . . I'll think of something." She sings "Female of the Species."

By some quirk of our genetics
Girls mature more quickly
Which spelt out in plain phonetics
Means that she must wait
'Till the boy she fancies
Starts to see her
As a woman . . .
When a woman
Takes a lover
Finds a man whom she adores

> Those who cross her
> Soon discover
> Little girls have razor claws

To further complicate things, Honoria Glossop, an intellectual Amazon, is after Bertie. By the end of the first act, Bertie finds himself engaged to three women in some rather devious plotting. The second act is filled with a wild series of farcical events in which Bingo Little also claims Honoria and is thwarted by the villain Spode who says he claims "everything"—evidently, in addition to Madeline. A wild tennis game is played (and sung) to the accompaniment of such lyrics as "the only way to play tennis, its service with a smile." And a free-swinging, mad fight brings us closer to the end—and some resolutions of love suits. Stiffy and Pinker are betrothed. Bertie "conquers" Spode by finding the magic word that calms him—"Eulalie"—in Gussie's lost notebook. And so Gussie will have his Madeline at last.

The final reprise of the opening number, "Banjo Boy," has a comic twist in that we have been waiting throughout the production for a broken string to be replaced. And when it finally arrives at the close, it is a muted string which will require Bertie to mime the sound which, of course, the audience will roundly hear. One last ironic comment brings us back to the stage within a stage set—"but the patron left with the critic."

Irving Wardle was one of the few critics who recognized the production as a resourceful and clever adaptation of Wodehouse, giving high praise to Ayckbourn while denigrating the uneven score.[6] Ronald Bryden was another who cheered Ayckbourn's book and lyrics and complained of the music ("the tunes themselves aren't bad, just misused"); and particularly, of the huge house, the spacious Her Majesty's Theatre ("four times too large for it"). Bryden praised the opening song, "Banjo Boy," for having just the right effect—"a heaven-made marriage of period Broadway zip and the Wodehouse world." However, he claims, "From there it goes downhill, mainly in a misplaced desire not to repeat itself. Having found its perfect idiom, it should have stuck to it . . . the rest of the music tries to offer orchestral equivalents of Wodehouse's prose effects—madrigals, summer-day pastorals, mock-romatic ballads." It should have, he concludes, stayed entirely within the spirit of 1920s musicals, such as *No, No, Nanette* or *Leave it to Jane*.[7]

Suburban Strains (1981)

The general view that many of the problems of the unsuccessful *Jeeves* were due to the difficulties of working with some one else's material seemed to be completely confirmed with the success of *Suburban Strains* five years later.[8] In this work nearly everything but the music is the work of Ayckbourn—books, lyrics, and direction. An earlier musical revue, with Paul Todd, *Men on Women on Men,* in the summer of 1978 in Scarborough, may well be a trying out of essentially similar material.[9] The common subject continues: modern day tribulations of very modern young men and women.

Carolyn, a school teacher in her early thirties, has enough emotional turmoil for them all: she is confusingly joined—legally married—to an actor of doubtful promise; and, as the play begins, they have separated and she begins a series of questionings, in song and without, about the life she leads and the better life she wants. Cleverly staged flashbacks together with a series of new encounters, which are even more clever when staged simultaneously, show us the full, engaging condition of her dilemmas.

The complete range of her strivings are first displayed when good friends, Jilly and Ivor (who call themselves "Bubbles" and "Bundle"), come to her "rescue" and call her back to life from two weeks of hiding in her apartment. Kevin has left. The characteristic Ayckbourn wry note is immediately sounded as Carolyn complains that the rescuing party in their own cooing and love protestations seem to be ignoring her: "How I wish," she sings, "they could be/more aware of me." While Jilly and Ivor croon their lovesong ("All for Love"), Carolyn bitterly admits, "Oh Dear God/How I hate/Other people's love." So many things seem to be wrong with her life; could it be that she is unable to have meaningful, loving relationships? Carolyn's plaintive song, "Carolyn's Questions," sung throughout the scene, runs the full gamut. Perhaps, she concludes, she's better off alone:

> That pathetic female sight
> Unapproachable by day
> And so alone at night

Time past and time present move smoothly back and forth in a succession of stage challenges completely suited to Ayckbourn's well-known fascination with the far limits of stage craft. The production probably has more scene changes than in any previous Ayckbourn play. A newly installed double revolving stage provides the answer; whatever is needed for the scene is quickly spun into place, actors and set pieces included. The result, according to nearly all the reviewers, is an entertaining, fast-moving musical play with appropriate songs falling just as easily into the appropriate places. Irving Wardle of the *Times* describes the process:

> Ayckbourn has mounted his production on two concentric revolves (a device I have not seen before), which not only secure speedy changes of scene and present the same scene from different angles, but also enable him to shuffle past and present in the bewildered Carolyn's mind: allowing her absent husband to walk through the set in the midst of a tender encounter with the new man; and showing her twice returning home from dinner parties to hold double conversations with the two men she brings back on the two different occasions. [10]

Carolyn's present confusion, following the departure of her husband, is further aggravated by the fact that the two had espoused an open liberal approach to their marriage: they were to take each other as they were—no changes. "As they were," however, becomes a nightmare for Carolyn; his sloppy habits became impossible for her. She is now unsure what to believe. Things at school are also not right; she is unsure how to handle the open idolization of one student, Linda. An older teacher, Miss Dent, begins to encroach on her privacy, a once unassailable province. As Yeats would say, "All things fall apart; the center cannot hold." In another flashback, Carolyn and Kevin sing in "Easy Come, Easy Go," of the once special conditions of their marriage:

> KEVIN. Marriages
> From the start
> Change your name
> Then your heart
>
> . . . .
> Our wedding was lover's leap
> With this ring I'll with thee sleep
> Love never came more cheap.
>
> CAROLYN. Please rush off if you feel the need to—
> Don't feel bound by all we've agreed to.
> What's an oath
> Here or there?

> Easy vow
> Easy swear.
>
> Off you go.
> Glad you came,
> There's your coat.
> Take your name.
> [What about our open pact?]
> . . . .

KEVIN.   As we are
          We will be—

CAROLYN. More of you—
          Less of me

KEVIN.   Love's a dance
          To and fro—

CAROLYN. One false step
          One less toe.

BOTH.   Easy come,
          Easy go.

KEVIN.   Here it comes.

CAROLYN. There it goes.

There is a marvelous, plaintive cry in all these simple declarations. And Paul Todd's music, according to the critics, remains "wholly self-effacing as a support to the action."[11] It was also to be expected that many would cite. resemblances to Stephen Sondheim, perhaps with the similar *Company* in mind. The stage can always benefit from another tale of modern-day unrest if the book and lyrics are incisive enough and the pace of the action is sufficiently engaging. Ayckbourn's many talents have an excellent chance here to accomplish both. A dinner party in which Carolyn meets the new man, Matthew, culminates with a clever long number, "Table talk," which is very much in the Sondheim and Noel Coward fashion, with excerpted bits of conversation pieced together to form a smart social smorgasbord. And later another suitor, Howard, though quite inept, joins with Carolyn and Matthew in a clever time-fused scene, singing of their common doubts:

> Here we are
> You and I

>Playing mating games
>Non-procreating games.

Things, however, soon come full circle with Carolyn's failed attempt to live another self, a less restrained self, with Matthew, the doctor. He begins to criticize her—her feet are wrong, "bottom's too big," color blind, nose wrong, ears crooked, "tits are lopsided," and her voice is squeaky. The parting blow comes when he gives her a book, *A Hundred Ways to Keep Fit,* plus a whole herbal beauty treatment. Finally, she must choose between the neatnik doctor and the rambunctious Kevin, husband *in absentia.* The choice becomes apparent as she sings to Matthew: "I'm an individual/You gotta take me warts and all." And in a quick whirlwind of recollected voices calling to her, she shouts her defiant testament of new self-confidence— "Me's all I've got"—and settles down with Kevin at the final curtain.

The critical response was generally favorable, even if at times overgenerous with the disastrous *Jeeves* in mind. The consensus seems to be that Ayckbourn deserves a modest place in the world of musical comedy, even if "the songs are the least important part" of the entire production.[12] What does matter, the *Observer* suggests, are the new directions in Ayckbourn's craft: "the form has released something in the playwright. . . . And though his subject matter remains much the same as before—loneliness and casual cruelty—the approach has opened up. He has tended before to show us relationships so far gone in decay that the participants are too tired to shift or too blind to notice. Here we see the rot starting, the characters struggling."[13]

Many, however, were quick to point out that Carolyn's "struggling" was rather arbitrarily worked out at the ending. Why, they asked, return to Kevin? Or even continue with the fastidious doctor? Why, after some success in finding herself—"I've got my faults," she concludes, "But they're the nicest part of me"—go with anyone? Nevertheless, the "artificially sweetened ending" remains, as Paul Allen points out, as a reminder that this is still fundamentally "good-time theatre" where the audience would rather be cheered than provoked when they leave the playhouse.[14] Ayckbourn's task then, which he eagerly embraces, is to keep the audience smiling while he tells his sometime troubled story of Carolyn, our liberated modern woman.

All in all, Ayckbourn has had fairly good success writing occasional

musicals. He particularly enjoys doing brief lunchtime revues with
Paul Todd, the company's musical director. Whatever pleasing results have followed have been due to the fortunate collaboration between the two. In contrast to the usual words-and-music method,
they work it the other way: first comes the music and then the lyrics.
With *Suburban Strains,* for example, Todd "was the last one to know
what the play was about. Ayckbourn would say, as it got later: 'I
think we need a big I-hate-you-and-I'm-leaving-you song, something
like . . . ,' and Ayckbourn would give him a rough lyric line; and
he'd bang out a melody for it."[15] The complete lyrics would then
follow.

Much of *Suburban Strains* developed from specific earlier revue ma-
terials, what Ayckbourn calls "one-act songs." These are actually
small one-act plays put to music. Ayckbourn could take Todd's music, say thirty minutes of a well-structured composition, and write a
one-act play on top of that. The results, in time, might be a kind of
"Music Theatre," as Ayckbourn sees it:

> Maybe it will have dialogue interspersed, or I may come back and say:
> "This tune's very successful, but I need it again, because this is the way the
> dramatic flow is going." I'll try, as far as possible, not to mis-shape his im-
> ages. So he's writing an overture . . . a sort of symphonietta. And that can
> only work really in the sort of theatre we're at, because he's taking a lot on
> trust. He's turning out thirty minutes of music which could finish up on
> the rubbish tip, if it doesn't work. But Paul's got a great generosity of mu-
> sic: if you ask for a tune, he'll give you nine.[16]

Ayckbourn likes to think that this interest in "musical writing"
nicely complements his play writing. His confidence in his ability to
do lyrics is greatly increasing. "Writing songs has been like using
other muscles—the ability depends on constant practice." "You
know," he confided to Ian Watson, "I could finish up being quite a
good lyric writer, if I keep at it long enough; and indeed, I'm learning about music. Not about chords and notes, but about what it does
to words, which is very important."[17]

Chapter Four

Relatively Speaking, "Countdown," How the Other Half Loves

Relatively Speaking (1967)

Rare as it usually is, nevertheless, everything was in his favor when Ayckbourn's *Relatively Speaking* opened at the Duke of York's Theatre on 29 March 1967.[1] It is remarkable to have a first West End success so warmly received. It is also marvelous to have a first-rate comedy that simply delights—that has nothing to sell—and is matchlessly performed by an excellent foursome, Michael Hodern, Celia Johnson, Richard Brier, and Jennifer Hilary. In the words of the *Times* drama critic Irving Wardle,

> *Relatively Speaking* is a single-minded contribution to the theatre of pleasure; and for once I am compelled to admit the existence of a good play that has practically nothing to express. Alan Ayckbourn performs over the old marital territory, but he has no point to make about adultery or erotic betrayal—least of all the implicit moral judgments which used to underprop commercial comedy. He tackles the theme simply as a game to be played as brilliantly as possible, and for once "brilliant" exactly describes the result.[2]

The mode is farce, and the plot moves along with an almost technical precision—and believeability. Ayckbourn has "a knack of construction," writes J. W. Lambert, "which makes each scene, each line even, a springboard to the next absurdity."[3] The structural requirements of proper farce are demanding, as Ayckbourn has acknowledged a number of times. However, he believes his natural style is farce, and farce demands movement: "Plays like *Relatively Speaking* are continually knotting and unknotting. There's never a moment when somebody isn't discovering or about to discover something."[4] What we all pleasantly discover in this play is that the

29

English have an incredibly delightful tolerance for polite misunderstandings. Chance meetings, unprepared encounters, which elsewhere in our modern life would be psychological disasters, are here blithely and courteously allowed. That is, they are "allowed" to continue (as the plot demands) far beyond the ordinary, eventual, full rational explanations. Good form, British style, seems to demand a steadiness of composure and reserve that can brave out anything, no matter how ridiculous or even absurd. In this sense farce becomes an almost natural British form of theater.

Greg and Ginny are a young modern couple, living together, who have arrived at that time in their relationship when a more lasting arrangement, marriage, is desired. To accomplish this, Ginny sets out for her former lover's home in the country to retrieve their letters. However, she pretends to Greg that she is going to her parents' home. Greg, a bit suspicious, follows after. In turn, each of them is welcomed into the country home, and a carefully involved series of misunderstandings is deftly played out. The tricks of the "game"— and our pleasure—is in the way the "parents," Philip and Sheila, inadvertently take up roles thrust upon them. Philip is the older ex-boss, who Ginny is trying to escape from; and Sheila, his wife, is simply—in the basic British manner—too polite to throw them all out!

For example, when the confused Greg makes his first appearance, he gains his entry by his partial answers to natural first inquiries. (*We know that he has come to ask the parents for Ginny's hand*):

GREG.   [*After a tentative pause*] Hallo.

SHEILA.   [*Startled*] Oh. Oh—Hallo there.

GREG.   Hallo.

SHEILA.   Are you—er . . .?

GREG.   I beg your pardon?

SHEILA.   Were you wanting to see someone?

GREG.   Yes.

SHEILA.   My husband?

GREG.   Not . . . altogether. . . .

SHEILA.   Me?

GREG.   Partly.

SHEILA.   Oh, well then.

What little is said is sufficient for the entry to be made and the misunderstandings to begin. In no time they are chatting away about delphiniums, and so forth, but every once in a while the "chat" abruptly halts and they quickly check each other as to who is who ("This is the Willows, isn't it," Greg asks), and then somehow the charade continues. Our delight is in watching the deft balancing act that farce demands in which truth and untruth somehow manage to side step each other.

While the so-called absolute truths are being jockeyed around, the always engaging relative truths are being warmly maintained in conversations that lead nowhere. The trick is to have the "private" remarks hold enough double meanings so that each believes what he wants to believe of the other. It is as if two people strike a bargain and each walks away, saying "Yes," "Yes"—and yet nothing is really agreed upon. When Greg and Philip finally have their talk, and Greg asks if he (the supposed father of Ginny) knows about the two of them, "me and her," Philip believes that he is referring to an affair between Greg and his wife, Sheila. He answers with a ready, "Oh yes"—and that allows the entire comic scene to be played out with each following his own truth of things.

Philip becomes quite intense about the wife whom he believes he is losing: "She costs me thirty quid a week to run and that doesn't include over-heads." When the suitor, Greg, presents the facts about his paltry income, it does startle Philip. He is even more taken back when Greg says that "she" has had other lovers—even "some bloke who's old enough to be her father." To Philip that means someone around seventy, which makes his wife Sheila even more of a remarkable mystery! Appropriately enough, the first act ends with Ginny arriving, again with the same tenuous but trusting reception by Sheila. All of this, of course, is very light stuff. "Gossamer" is the word B. A. Young uses: "The material it's made from is so flimsy that it's a wonder the piece holds together at all." But gossamer, he adds later, "has another quality; it glitters delicately and prettily in the light, and so does *Relatively Speaking*."[5]

The glitter continues in act 2 with the confrontation between Philip and his ex-mistress, Ginny. For the first time in the play we have the "novelty" of being with two people who really do know who and what they are talking about. No miscues here: Ginny is quite direct—she wants out of the affair. Philip still has ideas of maintaining his hold, but this becomes even more doubtful when Ginny in-

troduces him to Greg as her father—and, nonplussed, Philip has to
accept the charade.

Scene 2 of the second act presents a major challenge to the playwright since now everyone except Sheila "believes" the father-daugh-
ter business—and yet conversations with Sheila must still, somehow,
make sense. We run along this narrow edge for a little while, waiting
for the ultimate drop; and then, abruptly, Sheila says to Ginny:
"were you born in London or in the country?" Here, very wisely,
Ayckbourn reverts to stage business to save the day: Ginny chokes
terribly on her coffee and in the ensuing melee the question is for-
gotten. The situation remains, nevertheless, and Sheila finally blurts
out to Greg that Ginny is *not* her daughter. The farce formula—
which is well worked here—remains, however, to stave off the truth.
Earlier, Ginny had allowed Greg to assume that she was an illegitimate daughter. What follows now between the earnest Greg and the
confused Sheila is an excellent comic scene in which he berates her
"irresponsibility":

> GREG. It's about time you tried to come to terms with this, isn't
> it?
>
> SHEILA. I'm afraid I don't follow you.
>
> GREG. Why, why, why turn your back on it? Ignore something
> that happened over twenty years ago? What's the point?

Greg's "moral lesson" for Sheila is completely lost, however, since
she still has no idea what he is talking about. Four times she has told
this young man that Ginny is *not* her daughter, and the net result for
Greg is to believe that he is hearing a mother's adamant rejection of
her illegitimate child. The full comic force of the scene is made even
better by the two "joining in" in their sadness for the deplorable situation. Note in the following that Sheila's comments are simply polite interjections (basic English polite concern) in the most objective
sense:

> GREG. (*Getting excited*) What do you think it's like for a girl to grow
> up in this sort of atmosphere? No wonder she came near to
> ruining her life. With a father who's a moral schizophrenic
> and a mother who refuses to admit her existence at all.
>
> SHEILA. Oh, poor girl.
>
> GREG. Yes, poor girl.

SHEILA.   I didn't know. How terrible.

GREG.   You do see that, then?

SHEILA.   Oh yes. I do. No wonder.

GREG.   Yes.

SHEILA.   It is irresponsible, isn't it? People of that sort really shouldn't have children at all, should they?

GREG.   They haven't faced up to it, that's what it is.

SHEILA.   Indeed they haven't—

GREG.   You get what I'm driving at?

SHEILA.   Oh yes, I do. I do. I do.

GREG.   Fine.

SHEILA.   I'm not her mother though. [*Moving off terrace*] Please let's get that straight.

Eventually, everything turns out the right way: Greg goes off with his Ginny, and the scheming Philip is cowed by the wise and patient Sheila. One last bit of irony is the doubt in Philip's mind as to how many other men were his rivals during his affair with Ginny. Nevertheless, all the domestic circles—the proper ones that is—snap shut again; and at the curtain we are left peacefully in the country again waiting for the inevitable chain of overpoliteness, British reticence, and mistaken identities to play itself out again. Such is the charm of the well-wrought farce.

"Countdown" (1969)

"Countdown" is a one-act play, one of a number in an anthology of plays with other writers entitled *Mixed Doubles,* "An Entertainment on Marriage."[6] The novelty here is to have nearly all the dialogue consist of interior monologue reveries by the two principals. Whatever the husband and wife are to each other outwardly in their twenty years of marriage they are far more interesting to us in their spoken revelations of their true feelings. We have here a clever reversal of our usual open and contained lives. Many opportunities present themselves for comedy.

The scene is after supper with the couple reading the papers and arranging tea. We hear complaints from the husband about the paper being in the wrong order. He carries the tea trays in but observes that some men, when no company is present, "slam it in the wife's face." He gives an example of two-edged politeness: "We know all about Bert Evans. Held her chair for her the last time we were there. Took her so much by surprise she nearly fell on the floor." Other offerings from the husband ironically concern a yearning to cut grass—even though he neither owns a mower nor grass, except for a tiny patch.

An effective silent game ensues: he laughs, she laughs, and they are never entirely sure what the other thinks. Fundamentally, the husband has more somber thoughts as he recalls the better past and the bitter present. She looks terrible now, he says, like a bit of cake. "Dehydrated. All the goodness sucked out of her." Finally, the sketch ends with the husband telling a joke which the wife entirely misses.

How the Other Half Loves (1970)

The success of *How the Other Half Loves* depends on the cleverness of Ayckbourn's daring stage conception—two family settings literally superimposed upon each other.[7] Two pairs of actors walk deftly around each other playing out their own scenes unaware of the others. The fun, of course, is that *we* are tantalizingly aware of the trick, particularly when the two stories quickly merge along the lines of the standard farce. The set, therefore, demands a rather careful consideration. At first glance it appears to be a normal arrangement of a living room on one side and a dining room on the other. The entrance is in the middle upstage. However, on a closer look at the published sketch, we see that various pieces of furniture are marked for the respective family member. For example, the Foster sofa is handy to the Foster telephone, and the Philips chair handy to the Phillips telephone—all necessary for the somewhat tricky telephone business from one family to the other. The dining table chairs are marked the same way, with the additional clever business of having two swivel chairs for the guests who sit at two dinners at the same time—the tour de force of act 2.

In all other ways the play is rather standard farce with the expected mixture of cuckoldry, coverups, misunderstandings, and general mayhem. There are two families, the Fosters of upper management and the Phillipses at the middle level. Frank Foster, the mild-mannered executive, is continually behind the sequence of things, run hard though he might; he is the butt of many of the misdirections

off the required number. The Featherstones arrive—Mary, exceedingly shy and William a bit more confident—and are greeted in turn by Fiona and Teresa. Bob had previously stomped out of the house for the nearest bar upon learning what Teresa was up to. He accuses her of trying "to settle their marriage over dinner."

When Frank finally joins the guests, he adopts the playful posture of the "earnest suitor" after Mary's affections, a bit of misdirected lightness which completely befuddles the shy Mary. Frank shifts to another approach, plants himself between William and Mary on the couch, one arm around each, and proceeds in Dutch Uncle fashion to make a plea for marriage:

> You know, I'd like to say something to you both and—you can take it as you will. My wife and I . . . we've been married—well, it was our anniversary yesterday—for God knows how many years. And there are times when acrimony creeps in. In other words—we drive each other up the wall. And it is at times like these I say to myself, Frank, it's better than nothing. And the older you get, the better it is and the bigger the nothing. So my advice is, stick it out. Stick it out. Don't do things now that you're going to regret when you get too old like me to want to do them anymore. [*Pause*] And that's all I have to say on the matter. Cheers [*Toasts them*].

Matters now revert to the other dinner going on with the Phillipses. When William confesses to Teresa that he drinks sparingly, she is convinced now that Bob has been lying about his "evening out," supposingly consoling William at the bar. While the guests watch open mouthed, Teresa blithely puts Bob's dishes and silverware on a tray, goes to the front door and throws everything out. A bit wild by now, Teresa turns to the Featherstones and announces that, nevertheless, she will serve a nice dinner, that she will be "permissively modern" while "in the absence of our lord and master, who is probably groveling on the floor with some topless hostess by now."

As the Featherstones sit at the table—actually at two tables, they are in continual need of their swivel chairs. For example, everytime Teresa slams the kitchen door and returns to the table, the Featherstones quickly swivel to face her. And when that scene is over, they quickly swivel around to face Fiona or Frank Foster for another scene. Split second timing keeps the farce swinging back and forth—from Teresa's near mania to the extreme diffidence and politeness of the Fosters.

The evening finally reaches an uproarious ending with the return of the half-drunk Bob, now insulated against all further matrimonial adjustments with a coat full of beer cans. William backs away, resists the proffered beer, while Mary simply tries to hide somewhere from Bob's insistent greeting: "There's Mary the mouse. Hello Mary the mouse, how are you?" Teresa threatens violence as Bob continues to berate the guests. Finally she returns from the kitchen with the tureen of soup and, aiming at Bob, throws it on William instead. The Phillipses run out screaming at each other. The physical counterpart to William's adventures with the soup is provided for in the companion scene at the Foster dinner. There, his dowsing is explained by a leaking faucet in the upstairs bath, the faucet which has had most of Frank's attentions during the dinner in his inept attempts to be the "handy plumber."

The morning after.   The second act opens with familiar morning activities in both households—Frank jogging, Bob bleary eyed, searching for coffee. This time, however, the sign above the door accounts for Teresa: "Goodbye forever." She has left with the baby. Surprisingly, Mary arrives at Bob's to help out; she is following William's advice to get out and be more social. An amusing scene follows in which Bob frightens Mary by quickly accepting her solicitations and then ordering her to clean the house. All Mary can do is to retreat again ("I ought to go") as he advances on her with mop and bucket. He suggests they have an earnest, frank talk about their respective marriages. Mary inches closer to the door. Bob pulls his belt off and snaps it before her. Completely frightened by now, Mary screams, grabs the bucket and mop, and runs into the kitchen.

At the Fosters we find Teresa and the baby as early morning visitors. While Frank rambles on about this and that in his own home life he manages to reveal enough about Fiona's "missing act" last Wednesday night to ring the requisite bell with Teresa. She now knows about Bob and Fiona, and uses her advantage to drop a few cutting lines for Fiona's benefit—and bewilderment. More confusions follow befitting a farce: Frank calls Bob and on getting Mary instead assumes that these two are the lovers. He calls William to come to his house, supposedly to fix the drain. Back at the Phillipses, things have taken a different turn. Teresa has returned home. Somehow, they both turn on the hapless Mary. Bob complains of her dusting: "In five minutes you've undone years of her [Teresa's] work." Teresa complains that the change in her nice jumble of news clippings into a neat pile is outrageous. The Phillipses begin another round of fighting in which the obvious sexual overtones completely bewilder Mary. Finally, Bob throws Teresa over his shoulder and heads for another room. The verbal assault continues:

BOB.   You stupid bitch.

TERESA.   Dirty bastard. [*Just before they go into the kitchen—to Mary*] Honey, you won't wake Benjamin, will you?"

At the Fosters, similar dynamic events are about to erupt. William arrives and learns the "truth"—according to Frank—that Mary and Bob are lovers, and goes beserk. He raves about what he has tried to do for that girl, to bring Mary out, to make something of her: "Do you realize, Mrs. Foster, the hours I've put into that woman?" He rushes to the other house to have it out with Bob. One last wild scene follows with William's maniac attack on the hapless Bob. They fight. Mary screams as Teresa rescues the fallen Bob with one well-placed karate chop on William—and the curtain falls.

The final scene could be called the "reconciliation," as Frank gathers everyone in his home on the following Sunday morning. In quick order, the mistmatches are unmatched and some truth and order are restored. The meek Mary even secures an apology from husband William. When he begins to splutter and cough and cannot quite say it, the wiser Mary explains: "It's very difficult for him. You see, he's never been wrong before." All leave; and now alone with Fiona, Frank realizes that there is still one question unanswered. This time Fiona chooses the direct approach and disarms Frank completely by simply revealing the truth. The cleverness of the scene is in the fact that she says it in such a polite way that she draws out an equal politeness (the characteristic English diffidence) from the absentminded Frank. When she says, "It really wasn't anything. . . . He was really nothing compared to you," Frank is actually complimented—and forgives her. Shrewd to the last, Fiona withholds the man's name ("not important") and Frank accepts.

The critics.   Irving Wardle, writing in the *London Times,* conceded that everything in the play depends on "the manipulation of incidence." Unlike other comic playwrights who "hedge their bets" with "social relevance or psychological comment" when the laughs fail, Ayckbourn puts all his considerable effort into incident. "The fun he offers," continues Wardle, "is akin to watching a house of cards continually in danger of collapse."[8] The play was a great success in London, continuing for over two years. I have seen two productions, the original in London starring Robert Morley (Frank), and a college production in Rhode Island. I cite these two to indicate that the play as farce does not depend wholly on the expertness of the company to provide an entertaining evening. There is, in other words, certainly more to the play than what the cleverest professional company can bring out. At its base the play is essentially a series of very clever arrangements and incidents—all the handiwork of a crafty playwright.

There are a number of small effects which are deftly worked out by Ayckbourn for maximum humor. For example, in the first scene, Fiona attempts to place a call to Bob and is prevented when Teresa instead picks up the phone. At the same moment Frank returns to the room, so Fiona gives the time aloud as if she had just called for it—and hurriedly hangs up. At the Phillipses Teresa says a woman called.

BOB.   Woman?

TERESA.   Yes. Told me the time and hung up.

BOB.   Oh.

TERESA.   Aren't you supposed to call them?

BOB.   Usually. Was she abusive . . . made lewd suggestions?

TERESA.   No. She was a couple of minutes fast. . . .

This is a small moment, but it is effective and carefully arranged. There are other similar moments in the play, and the trick with Ayckbourn seems to be to rely on the sly recombination of apparently straightforward movements.

Clive Barnes, reviewing the New York production which successfully starred Phil Silvers as Frank, talked of "the theatrical adroitness of the author . . . which is as clever as tennis at its best."[9] On the other hand, Walter Kerr, while acknowledging the excellence of Silvers and Sandy Dennis (Teresa), considered the play only "a gimmick." "The error of the occasion," he maintained, "is the plot, which is simply a stock tale of suburban infidelity without any other comic nuance to put a gleam in its eye."[10] It could well be that the essential British character of the play was not apparent enough in the New York production, according to Kerr. Certainly, Kerr is thoroughly aware of those disarming mannerisms in theater which are characteristically British. Ayckbourn would be at a loss without them. *Relatively Speaking,* as we have seen, depends entirely on that singular British quality of politeness which seems to allow impossible situations to continue.

Everything about the upper-class Fosters depends on the couple's extreme genteelness. The condition provides exactly the right frame of basic ineptness and absentmindedness within which Frank can properly stumble. All the business, for example, about the electric toothbrush that he is forever trying to fix and the upstairs plumbing leaks, which he makes worse, serve to define an essentially British character. True, the comic elements are sufficient to apply anywhere; however, the difference here is that we have an automatic depth of characterization where ordinarily a stick figure would do as well. The very fact that Fiona is able successfully to "tell all" (up to a point) at the end of the play and get away with it is the clearest mark of the convenient genteelness and unflappability of the British.

Robert Morley. Doing *How the Other Half Loves* with Robert Morley, an established and singularly independent performer, was quite a lesson in theater for the young playwright. From the very start, the play became Morley's own vehicle, apparently to do with whatever he pleased. "He's an actor who rapidly gets very bored," Ayckbourn recalls, "and in order to refresh himself and to engage himself he always treats the theatre as one huge game organised by himself. The joy of the man is that he does have great enjoyment for what he does, an infectious, playful enthusiasm. Unfortunately, the people who suffer are the people who are on stage with him, or who are attempting to get on stage with him."[11]

There were obvious clashes between Robin Midgley, the director, and Morley. (As a very new young author, all Ayckbourn could do was "to sit rather quietly and weep in corners.") Morley actually saw himself as an actor-manager; he had strong views on how the other parts should be played. For example, his relationship to Fiona, his wife in the play, was not as Ayckbourn wrote it. The fact that Fiona is really a malicious character completely escaped Morley. She is meant to be faithless to her husband and to treat him with crushing sarcasm. "Robert insisted," according to Ayckbourn, "that anyone who was on stage with him should look as if they loved him." "Look," he would say, "nobody wants to come to the theatre and see people squabbling."[12] The fact that the center of the play does depend on some rather severely strained domestic relations somehow escaped him.

Nevertheless, as Ayckbourn is quick to admit, the overall experience taught him some valuable lessons about theater. Morley's interpretation of the play can surely be questioned, but he did do a masterful job in playing the part of Frank. True, it might have been better if he stuck to the script. The point to be made is that theater is an all-embracing art form which has room for a wide variety of entertainments. And Morley, in his own right, is an "entertainment." "You can't argue with the system," Ayckbourn concludes. "Eighty per cent of that audience had paid to see Robert Morley, and I, as an unknown dramatist, had really no right to stand between that process if I wanted to take the money."[13]

Such remarks also serve well to explain Ayckbourn's motives as a successful man of the theater. Whatever one might conclude about his farces, they do succeed admirably well in being what Ayckbourn seems to demand of theater—an evening's good entertainment with as little backstage strain as possible. Since he has always been involved with *all* aspects of the theater craft, it is difficult to accuse him of favoring the text (his own plays) over the sometimes competing "demands" of the company. Many times Ayckbourn talks of play material which will really challenge his ready company of actors, set designers, lighting technicians, and so forth. I believe it is important in our attempt to appraise Ayckbourn's work to keep in mind his unique position—in contrast to the majority of playwrights—as the director of productions in his own Scarborough theater.

Chapter Five

Time and Time Again
and Absurd Person Singular

Time and Time Again (1972)

When *Time and Time Again*[1] opened in London in 1972, J. W. Lambert said that Ayckbourn had bent the rules a bit and had written "a humanized farce."[2] He may well be right since the play is markedly different from the two previous successes (*Relatively Speaking* and *How the Other Half Loves*) in that we have a fully drawn, completely engaging kind of antihero in Leonard, the ex-teacher. In contrast to standard farce, we care almost as much about our hero's psyche as we do about the usual madcap events he gets into. It is, Lambert writes, "as if Chekhov had decided to write a burlesque version of Dostoevsky's *The Idiot,* and the whole thing had been adapted to the middle-middle-class suburbs of some English provincial town."[3]

The comedy takes place in the country, at the home of Graham and Anna, Leonard's sister, with the action in the conservatory, the back garden, and even a part of the adjoining recreation field. Everything about the Victorian terrace house and the garden is in disrepair. We see the small lawn, the old and tired lawnmower, and a murky pond with a small gnome statue as its intriguing—but prophetically sad—centerpiece. The principals have just returned from the mother's (Leonard's) funeral, and Leonard goes into the garden, and halfheartedly attempts to fix the mower and fails. To Graham's gruff remark that Leonard does not believe "in wasting time," Leonard calls attention to his brother-in-law's drinking: "It's a funeral you've been to, you know, not a launching." The wide, unimpassable gulf between these two is well demonstrated by the following brief exchange in which Leonard's characteristic tone is playful and Graham's, matter of fact:

LEONARD. [*Asked how they cut the grass in the Navy*] We used to paint it blue, instead.

GRAHAM.   Blue?

LEONARD. The grass. It was a secret Admirality device to run the en-
          emy aground.

GRAHAM.   [Puzzled] I never heard of them doing that.

LEONARD. It was just an experiment.

GRAHAM.   [Shaking his head] I never heard of that.

LEONARD. They had to abandon it eventually. It confused the R.A.F.
          When they flew over it, they weren't sure which way up
          they were. Half the bomber command were flying upside
          down at one time.

GRAHAM.   I don't believe that for a minute. You're making the
          whole thing up. That's a pack of lies.

LEONARD. That's just what the Air Ministry said.

Leonard and Graham are natural adversaries: Leonard ("a pale,
alert, darting sort of man") is sensitive, quixotic—always has a pat
for Bernard, the garden gnome—and exceedingly private; whereas
Graham is coarse, blustery, and seems to have a perpetual leer for a
pretty leg. His sensible wife, Anna, understands him too well and
continually acts as the buffer between Graham's gross limitations and
the real world. Graham's present "involvement" is with the young
and pretty Joan, fiancée of his employee, Peter. "Involvement" for
Graham, of course, means the usual sly tricks and risque remarks,
which flavor their afternoon tea together following the funeral. Obvious to all is that Graham is characteristically all smoke and no fire.

Leonard chooses to have his tea in the conservatory, since he has
been warned by Graham not to do a repeat of last week—not to "tell
his life story," and also "no more poetry recitals either." A clever
comic scene is established when Peter brings tea out to Leonard in
the glassed conservatory enclosure where they are still able to see and
react to the others in the house. Graham, alone with Joan, plays up
to her, pats her leg above the knee ("Some men have all the luck,
eh?"), and continues to bother her as she calmly protests. Leonard,
highly incensed, sees all of this and tries to alert Peter, but everytime
he calls his attention to it, Graham takes his hand away.

Peter admits, however, that he trusts Joan completely even if they
are apart a lot. He explains to Leonard that they must because "basically we're violently jealous people." Peter confides that he once had
to fight three rounds with a rival; and over Leonard's objections, says
bluntly that it settled things. There was no grudge; the man left the

country—he had the better reach. To illustrate, they spar a bit, and Leonard is easily convinced of Peter's athletic prowess. Long arms, he muses, would win all the girls, even if "not the usual dimension a woman looks for in a lover." Peter urges Leonard to join his cricket team but Leonard backs off, reminding him what he has taught— "English, history, religion, nature walks, no games."

    PETER.   Pity I can't persuade you to play cricket, though. You live practically on the field. All you've got to do is jump that fence. . . .

    LEONARD.   That's the bit that deters me.

For all his physical ability, Peter is, seemingly, prone to accidents, as the play bears out. He too tries his hand with the reluctant mower and gets his fingers jammed. Leonard frees him and sends him off into the house for some first aid. Leonard eventually finds himself alone with Joan in the garden, and introductions are made all around, including Bernard, the gnome. During their conversation, Graham sits in the window, munching a sandwich, and watching them like a hawk. Joan complains that he is always staring at her, even in church. Leonard has the ready answer to all this harassment; he smiles and waves to the bug-eyed Graham who can hear nothing through the glass: "Stop staring, you great bald headed twit." He even urges Joan, who catches the spirit, to stick her tongue out at Graham. She does—and Graham nearly chokes. Leonard rolls in the grass.

The hesitant hero.   Apart from the usual Ayckbourn suburban mishaps, the real attraction of the play lies in the character of Leonard. Here we have a genuine misfit, as a central character, someone so passive that he even allows himself to be locked out when he discovers his wife with another man. We find him in the play devoid of some of the usual life supports—without wife, three children, and job. And yet Ayckbourn makes Leonard a fascinating character to watch, as he wanders in his desultory way through his sister's home and garden, constantly setting his brother-in-law on edge; and—in his own inimical way—about to fall in love with Joan, the assumed "property" of another man, a very muscular other man, reportedly violently jealous. There are enough elements here for standard farce and, in addition, with some very skillful maneuvering on the author's part, some rare opportunities to search the mind of a hesitant hero, a kind of bumbling Hamlet in oversized cricket flannels.

In his quest of Joan, as the action of the play continues, Leonard

consents to join Peter's cricket team. Entirely out of character but
with a hang-dog persistency, he shows up with borrowed flannels to
do his bit in the adjoining recreational field. As created by Tom
Courtenay, the resultant picture of expert ineptness is marvelously
complete and, according to the critics, hilariously funny. As Felix
Barker of the *Evening News* wrote, "The line 'there is definitely something wrong with those trousers' is not exactly a dazzling epigram.
Yet it produces a gale of laughter."[4] Leonard tells Joan that if he does
appear ridiculous ("There's no need to laugh"), it is only for her. And
when he adds that he loves her, she puts him off by being whimsical.
"I don't know," she says. "It's a sunny day, the pollen count is high,
there's nobody else much around at the moment. . . . I don't know.
Your elegant flannels have gone to your head. . . ."

Nevertheless, Joan becomes sympathetic to Leonard's plight. She
hears the entire story of his marriage breakup. Of course, all these
signs of concern thoroughly confuse Graham, who watches them intently and keeps yelling to his wife, Anna, to witness what they are
up to next. "She was stroking his face," Graham reports, and is
hardly calmed when Anna reasons that she was probably applying sun
tan oil. The preparation for the game continues and Peter arrives
from the field (barely visible on stage) and says that Leonard is up
next. Leonard struggles awkwardly with his new studded cricket
boots and somehow manages, to the running accompaniment of
Graham's coarse jokes and Anna's encouragements ("he should always
wear white"), to go off with Peter to the game. A good comic scene
follows as the action is called offstage. Graham shouts, "Hit up,
Leonard!" and immediately they "bowl him" and he is out.

The new "lovers," Leonard and Joan, continue their conversation
while he stands in the field ("I'm deep extra cover"), and Graham
continues his mocking remarks: "They've put him there to try and
stop them breaking our windows." Added to the fact that he is the
reluctant cricketer is his absorption with Joan's warming remarks of
affection. The net result for the game, as we might expect, is that he
drops the ball when it comes his way. To make it even worse, he
distractedly holds the ball while telling Joan that he loves her. When
he finally throws the ball back on the field he hits Peter on the leg.
Graham, by this time, is a screaming idiot: he accuses Leonard of
"killing off his own team now." While Peter is eased off again for the
first aid, the lovers find themselves alone and frolicking in the pond.
As they playfully embrace and kiss, Graham abruptly returns and is

shocked again. Seemingly, successful amorous play is deeply immoral when *he* is not a party to it. The curtain descends on act 1 while Graham sounds the alarm again: "He's at it again. He's at it again. He's at it again. . . ."

Charles Lewsen in his *Times* review remarked on "the impressive technical achievement" of having the cricket game and the marriage proposal running together.[5] It is the sort of innovative challenge that Ayckbourn prefers. Succeeding plays will indicate that for the kind of complete theater man that Ayckbourn is, these are the technical problems that he warmly welcomes. The playing of two separate scenes with different characters on one ingenious set in *How the Other Half Loves* was merely the beginning for Ayckbourn. More wizardry is yet to come.

Marriage plans.   In the second (and last) act the intriguing characterization of Leonard as an hesitant Hamlet deepens. Months have passed and it is now autumn; our shy hero has a new job picking up leaves for the Park Department. The marriage plans with Joan go forward, despite the caution of the sister ("he should have a better job") and the heckling of the brother-in-law: "He doesn't need a wife, he needs a nurse." Nevertheless, the women talk of the future, the housing they will need and—not forgetting—the immediate need to inform Peter. Leonard shies away from this duty, says he does not want to upset Peter, and the remark upsets Joan, as it should. She presses the issue and tells him to change out of his work uniform, the park overalls, and tell Peter right now. Doggedly, Leonard resists; unpleasant things are best put off. And, anyway, if it must be done, "I can tell him about us in overalls."

Hints of the major impasse to come are evident in Joan's quandary and Leonard's highly individual behavior. He may be the conquering suitor but he shows little indication of taking full possession of the field. In fact, he seems to enjoy the secrecy, at least in reference to Peter. When Graham enters the discussion, and suggests that Peter will tear him apart, Joan defends Leonard, but has no success in getting him to speak for himself. All our hero can do is to nod agreement in a silent, perfunctory way. Joan becomes exasperated. Leonard has the simplest answer to Graham's charge that he does not really want to be domesticated: "I think I'll just go for a walk."

When the meeting finally does come about with Leonard and Peter, the full frustration of the issue is completely demonstrated. Theatrically, it is one of the cleverest scenes in the play. Ayckbourn arranges a full reversal of intentions between the two "adversaries." Although the device is a standard one in farce—the bumbling misunderstanding—there is a thoroughly familiar and unsettling reading of character that is closer to Chekhov than Feydeau. As soon as Leonard tries to begin the conversation about Joan, he is put off abruptly by Peter's flat refusal to talk about it: "I'd rather not . . . if you don't mind." Somewhat similar to Leonard's own complete involvement with his own world, the robust Peter unhesitatingly assumes that the broached issue is really Joan and himself.

When Leonard confusingly tries again, Peter turns sharply on him ("don't push me"), and by now Leonard is thoroughly quieted and resigned. Anna brings tea and exits. The two "adversaries" sit resolutely down, each apparently convinced of what he wants to believe. Although Peter's misunderstanding is plausible—actually, he believes Graham is the barrier between Joan and himself—Leonard's meek acceptance of a communication that doesn't exist is entirely unreal:

LEONARD.   Well. That's it.

PETER.   Yes. Seems to be.

LEONARD.   Glad it's cleared up, anyway. You've taken it—very well.

PETER.   [Still bitter] Hardly much choice, had I?

The resolution of the action in the final scene is consistent with the audience's growing acceptance of Leonard as one of life's charming but inept losers. He even goes one step further in his passivity by allowing Peter's misunderstanding to wreak a kind of curious justice on Graham's leering improprieties toward Joan. When Peter storms into the house convinced that Graham is the one who is stealing Joan away and asks Leonard what to do, all that Leonard can say is to mumble something about the two of them (Peter and himself) being really alike and that "we must stand up to tyrants."

Finally, when calm—and truth—is fully restored, Joan is thoroughly disgusted with Leonard for letting the charade continue. Obviously, very little is left in their relationship to salvage. Leonard's defense ("I was reading my book. I didn't really notice") is enough to send her packing. So much for the indecisive hero. Now left to themselves, Peter and Leonard sort things out along a sort of sporting world philosophy—it was a fair fight, both have lost. They talk earnestly of the approaching cricket game, and in their friendly jesting Leonard kicks Peter's ankle. Peter grits his teeth and manages a smile, "Nothing at all—just help me on. I'll be all right."

The audience's feelings about Leonard are necessarily mixed—again more appropriate to Chekhov than to farce. We are led to wonder about the type and not just the dancing figure. What about the Leonards of this world? "His inability to assert himself," Frank Marcus says of Leonard, "stems endearingly from a reluctance to hurt people's feelings, and the author rightly shows us that it is men like these who cause the greatest havoc."[6] It may well be that the "wreckage" following in Leonard's wake may be even more insidious if we accept Peter Lewis's view: "It is his ambition to fail dismally at everything. But his gift is to make everyone else's ambition fail dismally while he remains unscathed. He does it by simply not trying. It is a brilliant strategy."[7]

It is questionable as to how much depth Ayckbourn has built into the character of Leonard. The play may be more a "whimsical fancy" which did not rise very far—as John Russell Taylor sees it—rather than the comedy of philosophical significance that some of the critics were anxious for. According to Taylor, Leonard tries to be Jimmy Porter, but is not really up to it; "he is too soft and silly" to be another angry young man.[8] Ayckbourn, himself readily admits that he is not politically committed:

I'm the all time "don't know" really. I'm usually against whichever government is in at the time, simply because it often seems so incompetent. In general, I try to reflect the sort of people I know who are also a bit like this. They don't vote and they have wild prejudices occasionally which are not based on any deep-thought reason. . . . My characters tend to live rather day to day, which I think most people do. They are that great big body in the middle in this country who are don't knows.[9]

Absurd Person Singular (1973)

A number of critics were quick to point out that *Absurd Person Singular* is a sardonic parody of Dickens with a Christmas Past, a Christmas Present, and a Christmas Future.[10] In structure it certainly fits the same pattern, since each of the three acts is set in a different home at Christmas, last year, this year, and next year. But it is not a morality play of the good and the bad. Instead, we have the characteristic Ayckbourn display of middle-class misadventures, in which muddling through becomes a singular English way of life. At times hilarious and at times harrowing, the three acts are really three separate plays loosely held together by the holiday settings and the unique use of the kitchen. The inglorious kitchen becomes the fit platform for each of the three acts as we watch three married couples celebrate Christmas together. "Things go horribly wrong for the wives in particular, and it is part of the comedy's ingenuity [as John Barber points out] that we see each in her kitchen, the seething center of their lives."[11]

Ayckbourn tells us that he had long been concerned about offstage action, that is, to center the play away from its apparent principal setting. When he first began to write the play he set the action in Jane and Sidney's sitting room for the holiday party. "I was halfway through the act," Ayckbourn says, "before I realized that I was viewing the evening from totally the wrong perspective." Other members of the party were "far better heard occasionally but not seen. By a simple switch of setting to the kitchen, the problem was all but solved, adding incidentally far greater comic possibilities than the sitting room ever held. For in this particular case, the obvious offstage action was far more relevant than its onstage counterpart."[12]

The device was to work beautifully since we were able to exercise our imagination on *the* party in the sitting room while we watched the so-called after-effects (or side effects) before us—in the kitchen. Here, the industrious Jane is readying the kitchen for the festivities, becoming slightly maniacal about its cleanliness. She never seems to stop wiping while husband Sid—small, dapper, with an "unflappable manner"—oversees things like the admiral on the bridge. Dutiful Jane wants everything just right ("I don't want to let you down") since there will be people present who are important to Sid's work as a merchant.

Doors open and close, and we are aware of long silences from the other room, and then bits of conversation as the kitchen door opens again. Marion, a well-groomed grand dame, comes sailing into the kitchen and is overwhelmed ("gorgeous . . . enchanting") with the standard equipment of the kitchen. This is an excellent comic scene. She tells her unmoved husband, Ronald, a banker, to try the cupboard doors—"so easy . . . lovely deep drawers"! She is the touring dilettante, as if she has never seen a kitchen before. And the fawning Sidney plays right into the act and gives a long litany of all the household aids he has constructed. Marion prattles on; Ronald becomes more bored than ever.

Farce has its chance in the troubles of Jane who runs out in the rain to get some tonic water. While Sid is confusingly trying to relate to Eva, a guest who cannot exist without her pills ("one's sanity can

depend on these"), Jane is at the back door, locked out in the pouring rain. She motions frantically but Sid fails to see her. She is finally
forced to reenter the house through the front door and the sitting
room, which shocks Sidney. He insists she go back in and apologize
for her ridiculous appearance since she is wearing some out-size rain
gear. Jane refuses and rushes out into the rain again as half-tipsy
Ronald enters the kitchen. Did you, he asks Sidney, see the "little
short chap" who ran through the room? Again, this is excellent farce
material.

I would, however, heartily agree with a number of critics who
chose the second Christmas as the funniest in the play, and perhaps,
I would add, one of the best acts in the Ayckbourn canon. This time
we are in the kitchen of Geoffrey and Eva, an untidy place with an
always lived-in appearance you could call "trendy homespun." Eva is
at a table in a dressing gown, unmade, unkempt, baggy-eyed, trying
to write a note with scraps of other trial notes on the floor. Geoffrey,
an architect with "moving plans," enters and continues in a long
monologue with a conversation which must have begun earlier in the
morning, around 4:00 A.M. He reminds her that they agreed that he
should move out and live with Sally. Eva will pull herself together
and everyone will become great adult friends. But right now, he reminds the silent Eva, they are having a Christmas party tonight.
During this long harangue, Eva says absolutely nothing. Geoffrey reminds her that they are *her* friends, the worst of them being the up-
and-coming Sidney Hopcroft, whom he refuses to work for with his
squalid new developments. "What I lack in morals," Geoffrey
smugly concludes, "I make up in ethics."

Geoffrey leaves but then quickly returns, having had another losing
tussle with their recalcitrant dog, George. At this point, he is angry
at everyone:

> Eva—I'm being very patient indeed. But in a minute I clearly do believe
> I'm going to lose my temper, and we know what happens then, don't we?
> I will take a swing at you and then you will feel hard done by, and by way
> of reprisal, will systematically go around and smash everything in the flat.
> And come tomorrow breakfast time, there will be the familiar sight of the
> three of us, you, me, and George, trying to eat our meals off our one sur-
> viving plate.

What makes this scene work so well is the realization that the pathetic Geoffrey fails entirely to realize how utterly devastated his wife

really is. In fact, none of the guests who will wander into the kitchen will realize that she is trying, without success, to kill herself. She finally finishes what is really a suicide note, fastens it to the table with a kitchen knife, and climbs out on the window ledge. Geoffrey, in the meantime, is running back and forth finding glasses for the guests, and half senses what Eva is up to and brings her in. Undaunted, Eva picks up the bread knife, walks to the drawer, and wedges it in the half opening, point out. She begins to run toward it but is intercepted by Geoffrey who catches her, still not entirely certain what is going on. Nevertheless, he will call a doctor.

The compulsive cleaner. Eva gazes around the kitchen, determined to find a way to end it all. She empties the oven, which is expectedly very dirty, lays a tea napkin down inside, and tries laying her head on it for size. This proves uncomfortable; she wriggles about, trying to find a better position. Jane, the compulsive cleaner, enters and believes that the ill Eva is trying to clean her oven, something she would never do even if well. But Jane, true to character, misreads the symptoms entirely and says she understands the feeling, the great impulse to clean it:

Now you sit down here. Don't you worry about that oven now. That oven can wait. You clean it later. No point in damaging your health for an oven, is there? Mind you, I know just what you feel like, though. You suddenly get that urge, don't you? You say, I must clean that oven if it kills me. I shan't sleep, I shan't eat till I've cleaned that oven. It haunts you. I know just that feeling. I'll tell you what I'll do. Never say I'm not a good neighbor—shall I have a go at it for you? How would that be? Would you mind? I mean, it's no trouble for me, wouldn't you? Right. That's settled. No point in wasting time. Let's get down to it.

While Jane prattles along deep inside the oven, Eva tries pills next. She swallows some, and accidentally spills others into the sink. Sidney enters, angry at his wife's unseemly "employment" in the oven, and mistakes Eva's groping with a fork in the sink for a stopped drain. The handyman in Sidney rushes to the surface and he offers to unblock the drain. His tools are in the car. Before he leaves, he draws a diagram of the problem on the back of the unread suicide note. "It's at times like this," he comforts the blank staring Eva, "you're glad of your friends, aren't you."

What makes all of these absurd actions work so well is Ayckbourn's fine awareness of the business of farce. Here the author, as

Robert Cushman points out, "blows up a real storm. He has taken the textbook maxim that the true mother of farce is desperation and extended it to its logical limit." And the process works beautifully, with "the broad contrast between the silent hostess, intent on self-destruction, and the noisy bonhomous guests."[13] Both go in entirely opposite directions—the hostess and the guests. It is almost as if we have a sightless world with no possible awareness of what the other is doing. The guests have their own individual involvements; and when they meet the groping suicide-mad Eva, they quickly read into the situation whatever fits their own interest. This is a fine, if mad, example of a world without communication. Jane has a mania for cleanliness, Sidney for his handyman abilities—and they automatically fall back into their myopic endeavors as substitutes for real human concerns.

The beauty of Ayckbourn's conceptions is that behind all the zany actions there are often major revelations of our basic human ill behavior. The second act succeeds because we have already had a full "reading" of the principals in the first act. We know them quite well. What can be said of Jane and Sidney in the second act can be applied to the others in the entire play: "Because they are terrified of doing anything wrong socially, everything does go wrong."[14]

The full farcical nature of the act builds to a wild climax with Eva's problems in trying to hang herself from the kitchen ceiling light fixture. She pulls the fixture down—and again a misreading of the situation; the others believe that she is changing a bulb. By now Sid has his large bag of tools, and he draws more diagrams (on another suicide note) on how the fixture should be wired. The situation now looks like this: Jane still in the oven, Sidney under the sink, and new accomplice Ronald working on the light fixture. Marion, with more than a few drinks, comes in and leads the ensemble of workers, pouring another gin for herself and Eva, who was about to drink some paint stripper out of a tin she had struggled to open. Ronald has trouble with the fixture, loses a piece, all grope for it, and Marion switches on the light, which sends Ronald vibrating on top of the table. There is enough mayhem here for a dozen scenes.

The third and final act takes place in the kitchen of the Brewster-Wrights—Ronald and Marion. It is a year later—"Next Christmas" the act is titled. We learn that circumstances have worsened for some of the three couples and improved for others. Here in a palatial but freezing kitchen things are not well for banker Ronald. The heating

system has failed and his alcoholic wife, Marion, is upstairs surrounded with electric heaters. The fashionable ones, Eva and Geoffrey, have their own problems; Geoffrey bristles when the now
recovered Eva suggests that he ask Sidney for help. "Darling," she
says "I hate to remind you but ever since the ceiling of the Harrison
building caved in and nearly killed the manager, Sidney Hopcroft is
about your only hope of surviving as an architect in this city." It
seems the up-and-coming Sidney is now a rich property developer and
universally disliked.

His eventual arrival with Jane, both in evening dress and wearing
funny hats, does little to please the company. Finding Ronald and
Marion (now below) bewailing their present anger at life, they set
about with a vengeance to cheer everyone up. "Can't have all these
glum faces," Sid announces as he starts a series of party games, which
quickly build to more and more ridiculous postures, antics, and even
embarassing forfeits. This final scene is amazingly effective in having
us "join" with Sidney in his vengeful ridiculing of the other couples.
As Ayckbourn himself admits, these final moments make the entire
play "a bit sour": the action of the game moves faster and faster ("ap-
ple under the chin . . . orange between the knees . . . spoon in the
mouth") until finally our laughter gives way to the full sober realization that an essentially cruel Sidney is whipping his charges around
("Dance. Come on. Dance. Dance. Keep dancing. Dance . . .") as if
he were the lion tamer in the cage. And the pathetic part is that the
others—Ronald and Marion, Geoffrey and Eva—now have no choice
but meekly to comply. All of this amounts to a startling comment
on business success. However, since the business of the play always
peaks at a farcical pace, we still leave the theater smiling, despite the
obvious opposite undercurrents.

Many of the critics held that the generally sober atmosphere of the
third act, that is, before the final whirlwind end, was disturbing.
Michael Billington referred to it as "total Strindbergian gloom."[15]
Robert Cushman pointed out that here "the action begins, fatally, to
slow up. Everyone gets contemplative."[16] It is of interest to add that
the New York producers began to worry about the change of tone in
the last act compared to the riotous laughter of the second act. Ayckbourn reports that they "even went so far as to suggest that it might
be a better play if the acts were played in a different order! They became neurotic over the fact that the play turns dark in the last act.
Glum messages would arrive reporting that 'the humor's going out of

it, Alan.' "[17] They even sent a tabulated laugh count for the acts. Ayckbourn, of course, refused to alter anything, it being obvious that the producers had missed the essential plot, which demands a distinct progression and development from one act to another over the course of three Christmas celebrations.

The antics of the first two acts—particularly the widely admired second act—properly prepare us for the state of affairs that close the play. And there is no doubt that the audience is easily pulled along on a high hilarious wave by the time act 2 ends. "An audience laughing themselves silly," as Janet Watts points out, "can be crept up on unawares with hard truths."[18] The generally acknowledged absurdity of suburbia suits Ayckbourn's method perfectly. "I don't want people to watch the plays," Ayckbourn tells us, "with their minds closed. I've a feeling that most of us today have to save ourselves, a cut-off point because we're exposed to so many terrible things in depth." What saves us is "the laughter of recognition."[19]

Chapter Six
The Norman Conquests (1974)

Ayckbourn's accomplishments with the much praised *The Norman Conquests* are quite impressive.[1] Apart from the many awards that followed is the singular fact that he has structured a play (or a series of plays) in a manner never before done in theater history! We have already seen a number of demonstrations of Ayckbourn's love for ingenious stagecraft, so it probably comes as no great surprise that sooner or later he would manage to top them all. What we have here is not the conventional sequential trilogy of plays but essentially *one* play told from *three* vantage points. In a word, each play is the offstage of the others. This we know is an interest begun, as he tells us, with *Absurd Person Singular* of the previous year. An intriguing question in theater is posed: what happens when the actors leave the stage action and go, apparently, into other rooms offstage? Ayckbourn has worked it out so that each play can be seen on its own, although with the same characters and with the same resolutions at the end. Each play will provide the same "information"—if that can be the proper word for the total accumulation of fascinating and entertaining insights into the lives of the six characters. Of course, the ideal arrangement would be to see all three plays, but even here the precise order of viewing does not have to be followed.

The way in which everyday life affects art—and ultimately gives it its proper form—is always an engaging story. At times, having the high mysteries of art reduced to the mundane is quite an unsettling experience. Some critics, admiring Ayckbourn's novel form, may have supposed that it was derived from a careful study and consideration of the trilogy form. Ayckbourn tells us that the plan was simply a theater expedient for his Scarborough resort audience who were not likely in their limited holiday plans to want to spend three nights in his theater. (After all, bingo deserved equal time.) And yet he wanted the "challenge . . . and the adventure for the actors and for me as director. Certainly, I never dreamed they [the plays] would be produced elsewhere. Trilogies, I was informed by my London sources as soon as the news leaked out that I was writing one, are not Good Things for the West End." Each play, therefore, had to stand independently—"yet not so much that people's curiosity as to what was happening on the other two nights wasn't a little aroused."[2]

A number of conditions had to be held to. No more than six actors could be used since that was all the company could afford. Other minor preconditions for all three of the plays had to be followed, but Ayckbourn readily admits that he is the kind of worker who thrives on working under a series of preconditions. The rapid, forced way he writes all his plays is witness enough. Once a year he hides himself away, and after a period of so many days and continuous nights he emerges with a finished script. *The Norman Conquests* took eight days in the spring of 1973. The process, as with the entire plan, was to be quite ingenious:

> Anyway, once I had sorted out the pre-conditions and was unaware that the scheme had few precedents, the problem of how to write it arose. . . . Since many of the actions within the plays had to cross-relate and, more important, since each character's attitude and development had to fit in with the general time structure, I decided in the case of the *Norman Conquests* to write them crosswise. That is to say, I started with Scene One of *Round and Round the Garden,* then the Scene One's of the other two plays and so on through the Scene Two's. It was an odd experience writing them, rather similar to Norman's own in fact. I found myself grappling with triplet sisters all with very different personalities.[3]

The Trilogy

The three plays are titled *Table Manners,* which takes place in the dining room; *Living Together,* in the sitting room; and *Round and Round the Garden,* obviously in the garden. The beauty of the overall title, *The Norman Conquests,* is that it teasingly does not refer to the conquest of England in 1066, but instead is an accurate reference to the amorous intentions of Norman, the assistant librarian, toward all three of the women in the play—one alone being his wife. Norman is one of the truly great characterizations in the Ayckbourn canon. He has an entirely singular—and basically harmless—way of doing things. Nevertheless, he is one of those unheroic heroes of modern suburbia who will continually complicate other lives. Ultimately, his defense will always be the much stated "I only wanted to make you happy," which fittingly closes each of the plays.

His great, endearing quality, of course, will be his independent
spirit, his wholly natural—sometimes naive—way of dealing with the
cumbrous details of modern civilization. He is a Don Quixote in new
pajamas. To all the others in the play "Norman commands central
position as the wild card to the pack. The other characters, with their
families, mortgages and job prospects," Irving Wardle points out,
"are simply too lumbered to move. Norman is there to try and infect
them with his own escapist fantasies, and to smash things up. He
always fails, but never admits defeat. That is the comic main-
spring. . . ."4

The plot is quite simple. A family gathers for the weekend at the
invalid mother's house, watched over by Annie, a young spinster.
The visitors include Ruth, an older sister, wife to Norman; and the
older brother, Reg, and his wife, Sarah. Tom, the local veterinarian,
completes the cast of six. We never meet the mother, but her demanding presence on the floor above provides some comic moments.
On this particular summer weekend they have gathered to relieve
Annie, who has planned a few days away. Complications begin when
we learn that Annie's recuperative weekend away is to be with her
brother-in-law, the inimicable Norman. *Table Manners,* the first play,
opens with the arrival of Sarah and Reg. It is during Sarah and Annie's long and strained greeting that the terrible truth about Annie
and Norman emerges. It would probably be more accurate to say that
in the comic series of statements the truth finally *descends* upon Sarah
like a thunderbolt:

ANNIE.   You don't think I should then?

SARAH.   What?

ANNIE.   Go.

SARAH.   Go where?

ANNIE.   This weekend.

SARAH.   This weekend?

ANNIE.   with Norman? to East Grinstead. [*A pause*]

SARAH.   You were planning to go with Norman to East Grinstead?

ANNIE.   Yes, he couldn't get in anywhere else.

SARAH.   You're not serious?

ANNIE.   Yes.

SARAH.   But how could you even think of it?

ANNIE. He asked me.

SARAH. What has that got to do with it?

ANNIE. Well, I wanted a holiday. . . .

SARAH. Yes but—this wouldn't be just a holiday—I mean, I mean, you just don't go off on holiday with your sister's husband.

ANNIE. It was only a weekend. I needed a holiday.

Annie's ingenuous tone is a favorite Ayckbourn characteristic; the marvelous innocent quality is the best foil when contending with figures like Sarah who continually see the world as a monstrous quagmire. Always complaining of the suburban rat race with her children and a somewhat vacuous husband, Sarah fits the label of one critic—"an all devouring Home Counties martyr." She had managed earlier in this initial conversation with Annie to draw out the relevation that last Christmas Norman had already "succeeded" with Annie. There they were, Annie relates, inadvertently alone in the house—and "it was just wham, thump and there we both were on the rug." The comic vein is well maintained with Sarah demanding to know which rug. As for the tryst with Norman, that is undecidedly out of the question even if she has no love for Ruth, the apparently injured party.

In their first remarks about Annie's planned holiday, Sarah had been hoping it might be Tom she would be with. Slow moving Tom is the inevitable hanger-on about the place. Little future here, as Annie puts it: "All that happens is that Tom comes round here like he has done for years. I feed him. He sits and broods. Sometimes we talk. That's all." Tom is another excellent portrait in the Ayckbourn gallery—well meaning but nearly one hundred percent certain to miss every point. Somewhat bearlike in his hulking presence, he seems hopelessly alien to real human concerns and emotions. His stock response to the many irritations in Annie's life is for her "to put her feet up"!

Events settle down, as they usually do in the Ayckbourn plays, to a series of comic blunders. Here, however, with a full set of extremely engaging characters, we have superb theater. The fact proves again that excellent farceur that Ayckbourn is, he is at his best with fully realized characters as complete and real to us as any in Chekhov's own similar domestic gardens. Trivialites overlaced with commonplaces can be a seedbed of comic possibilities when the mix of

characters is right. Playful, zany Norman has a field day when he is
finally introduced to the play. It is breakfast time, Sunday morning;
and since everyone by now is aware of his failed plans with Annie,
they are disinclined to say very much. But the ebullient Norman has
enough words for everyone as he prances—and prattles—over the
breakfast table. His three-page monologue, perhaps the longest in
Ayckbourn, is a masterpiece. Primarily a jesting defense of his actions, it serves most of all to introduce the remarkable Norman to
the play.

Don't speak. I don't care. Going to be a pretty dull holiday if we all sit
in silence. I can tell you. Well, I'm not sitting in silence. I'll find something to do. I know. I'll go up and frighten Mother.'. . . I suppose you
think that I'm cruel too, don't you? Well, I've a damn good cause to be,
haven't I? I mean, nobody's thought about my feelings, have they? It's all
Annie—Annie—Annie . . . what about me? I was going to give her everything. Well, as much as I could. My whole being. I wanted to make her
happy for a weekend, that's all. I wanted to give her. . . . [Angrily]. It was
only for a few hours for God's sake. Saturday night, back on Monday morning. That was all it was going to be. My God! The fuss.

The Amorous Librarian

The rejecting silence continues, but as Norman goes on he reveals
key, essential traits: he is a man born out of his time, he is a man
with much love to give; there is enough for *all* and his wife, although
Ruth clearly does not need him. It is a fine, impassioned plea, inter-
woven with wild, humorous lines ("What's inside you, Reg? Apart
from twelve bowls of cornflakes?"). Ruth, who was not expected to
be part of the weekend due to a very demanding job, arrives in answer to Sarah's midnight call. Ruth does not know why: "She [Sarah]
sounded as if she was summoning relatives to your bedside." Their
relationship offers another engaging mix of strained, half-comic ap-
peals, many nonsequiturs; and at times, not much more than general
confusion. Norman feels compelled to tell her the truth; and when all
of it is finally blurted out—in company with her characteristic pre-
possessive interjections—Ruth can do no more than break out into
uncontrollable laughter. Perhaps, it is the East Grinstead rendezvous
site that triggers it off.

Act 2 is the same evening with preparations underway for the family dinner, hopefully the quiet calming event Sarah sternly demands

from everyone. "Everytime I come down here," she reminds them, "I have a relapse. When I get home from this house, I find I'm shaking all over. For days. And I get these rashes up the insides of my arms." This is enough of an indication to us that what will follow, considering Ayckbourn's fondness for hilarity at mealtime, will be another comic classic. The managing Sarah takes full command of the arrangements, sending the others off to find enough unbroken chairs for the table. There are also the additional problems of the proper seating and the ever-changing order—where should the hostess sit? Can't have two women together?—and on and on, as the six of them keep changing places while Sarah issues commands. This is farce at its best as the tension rises. When the seating is finally completed, we find that not only is it without pattern—all three men on one side—but Tom is next to Norman in a very low chair. For the rest of the evening Norman refers to him ("Hallo, little chap") as a toddler, while Tom is forced to have his dinner at chin-high level to the table. Dishes, glasses, the salt, are passed over his head: "Here we are, little fellow," Norman says, "You enjoying eating with the grown-ups, are you? Long past your bedtime."

The evening (and the scene) comes to a noisy close with issues being raised between two natural antagonists—Ruth and Sarah, the career woman and the martyred homemaker. Ruth accuses Sarah of complaining too often of the difficulties of raising children ("If you didn't want children, you shouldn't have had them"). Sarah's rejoinder implies that a woman is incomplete without children. The anger and differences mount, and only other diverting actions prevent an open fight. One of these actions is a heated argument between Ruth and Norman which has its own conclusion with Tom striking Norman, wrongly believing Annie is being insulted. By the end of the scene, we have the remarkable circumstance of the two misunderstood "victims," Sarah and Norman, comforting each other.

This amazing turn around is neatly (and craftily) completed in the morning farewells. Characteristic of the open-hearted Norman is the way he supplies all his soothing gifts to the wounded Sarah. The approach is faultless—he "defends" her having children as a "miracle"—and in the best bedside manner begins to win her over on rather familiar lines: "When did you last have a holiday?" It is incredible that Ayckbourn manages in a series of clever lines to have Norman suggest a kind of "Annie holiday" for Sarah and himself—and that Sarah may accept!

SARAH.   When you mentioned about this holiday? Did you want to take me away just for my health?

NORMAN. Well, that came into it. There might be any number of reasons. I'm easy. [He smiles]

SARAH.   So long as I know. [She smiles] . . .

SARAH.   Reg gets home about half-past six in the evening on weekdays.

NORMAN. Busy man.

SARAH.   If you feel like giving me a ring anytime. I'm usually tied to the house. I don't get out much.

NORMAN. I'd make you happy, Sarah.

SARAH.   Yes.

The second play, *Living Together,* opens the same way with the arrival of Sarah and Reg and Norman for the weekend. The dovetailing with the first scene of the other play is quite exact since the opening action here involves reactions to the already revealed (and foiled) plot of the Norman-Annie weekend. It is neatly done with a reference to the game which Reg brought with him, one of his own making. "Norman can play" Reg suggests and Sarah quickly counters with, "I should think Norman's had enough of games, haven't you, Norman?"

Left alone, Sarah and Norman have the full confrontation on the sordid scheme. Norman's defense is characteristically aimless and innocent: "She wanted to come. I wanted to go. . . . She's stuck here, all on her own, day after day looking after that old sabre-toothed bat upstairs." He tells Sarah that he loves Annie, something that she cannot comprehend ("Don't be ridiculous. You're married to Ruth"). But his quick reply fazes her even more—"What's that got to do with it?" Their continual cross purposes reveal the real and the romantic. Sarah is mired down in the literal and the mundane. Even in the matter of Annie's appearance, she severely questions Norman's designation of Annie as beautiful. To Norman, Ariel incarnate, there is no issue: "Anybody I love is automatically beautiful."

The high point for comic hijinks will be the playing of Reg's home-made board game. (Games of all kinds have always been Ayckbourn's passion. The intricate working out of some complex play structure, as many critics have pointed out, often parallel Ayckbourn's own home amusements.) However, what transpires now is an

attempt on Reg's part to explain the game while at the same time
Norman talks to Ruth on the phone. It is another clever farce piece
with Sarah continually urging Reg "to get on with it," and Tom always unsure if he has it right. The game involves police chasing
crooks; the police cars move one way and the Chief "can see up to
three spaces ahead of him and three spaces round a corner." Sarah
calls it all absurd: how can a man do that?

REG.   Because he's got a very long neck. I don't know, it's a game
         woman.

SARAH.   It's not even realistic.

REG.   What's that got to do with it?

SARAH.   It's not much of a game if it's not even realistic.

REG.   What are you talking about? Realistic? [*Leaping up*] What
         about chess? That's not realistic is it? What's wrong with
         chess?

SARAH.   Oh well, chess. . . .

REG.   In chess you've got horses jumping sideways. That's not re-
         alistic, is it? Have you ever seen a horse jumping sideways?

SARAH.   Yes, all right. . . .

REG.   [*Leaping about*] Like this. Jumping like this. That's very re-
         alistic, I must say.

SARAH.   You've made your point.

Act 2 continues the hectic weekend, giving us the somewhat "ad-
jacent" scenes to the other plays. It has all been worked out with a
fine discretion so that both audiences—those who see only this play
and those who have seen others in the trilogy—will be satisfied. For
one there will be the complete integration of a whole, understandable
play; and for the others, who have already met the six characters,
there will be a satisfying extension, or filling out, of actions they have
already experienced. The net result will be a pleasurable—and so-
bering—involvement with a good stretch of the suburban human
condition, as major a subject for full investigation as any in modern
life. "Ayckbourn's world," as Bernard Davies wisely points out, "is
inhabited by people who are bound to each other not only by ties of
blood and marriage but also by what seems to me a rather dreadful
understanding of each other."[5] Toward the end of *Living Together*
Ayckbourn manages to bring Ruth and Norman together; and it may

well be that not too far below the comical devices that make it happen, there is a real "dreadful understanding of each other." Of course, the beauty of learning all this in an Ayckbourn play is always the laughable way we can accept ourselves, which is the true essence of universal comedy. True, there are other, well-known ways in literature, to the same end, but the comic way will always be a singular accomplishment.

Annie in the Garden

The third play, *Round and Round the Garden,* has some outstanding accomplishments. If we view the play from the vantage point of those who have seen the other two, we realize how truly satisfying it can be. The word "offstage" begins to mean something here since other aspects of the same situations have been played before—elsewhere in the house. But now the third-time audience member has a number of chances to actually *witness* what he had only supposed before. All the imagined scenes spring to life in this play. The process is an act of corroboration to the imagination. For example, even though much is already known about the secret weekend, we have not yet had a view of the matter from Annie, that is, a view that really completes our understanding of the woman.

Annie and Norman converse in the garden, Annie still mystified why Norman arrived here when they had plans, made six months ago, to meet in town. She attempts, in so many words, to rationalize their daring act: "We're being terribly adult, aren't we? You said we were—in your letter. . . . Far better we two just go away quietly to a little hotel somewhere, get it all off our chests—out of our system—God I'm making it sound like a laxative." If Annie has doubts, she is still generally persuaded by Norman's ineffable charms. In the following exchange we see how the lovers view each other:

ANNIE.   Oh Norman. . . . When you look like that, I almost believe you. You look like a—what are those things. . . ?

NORMAN.   Greek Gods.

ANNIE.   Old English sheepdogs.

NORMAN.   Oh great.

ANNIE.   They're super dogs. All wooly and double-ended.

NORMAN.   I'm not wooly and double-ended.

ANNIE.   You are a bit. You're like a badly built haystack.

NORMAN.   I'm going.

We are not surprised that it is nearly impossible for Annie to take
Norman seriously. Most of their time together is a confusing mixture
of self-fury and laughter. You might say that she desperately wants
to believe what the playful Norman is already convinced of, that
there still is romance in this world—despite "the cynics and libera-
tionists"—and that he is the *one* person who can bring it into their
lives.

Scenes played between Tom and Norman and between Reg and
Norman present more interesting aspects of Annie's difficult situation
in the house and her need to get away. As yet, Tom and Reg do not
know who her weekend "liberator" is. Tom even wonders if he should
offer to accompany her, an idea Norman quickly squelches. Reg, the
estate agent, talks of his sister as if she were a property up for sale.
But he does it kindly ("Not a great beauty, but her heart is in the
right place. Easy temperament, good around the house . . .")—all
good considerations when they question Tom's fumbling intentions.
In summary, by the end of act 1 Ayckbourn accomplishes further remarkable things for the good intentioned Norman. Somehow ("I'm
full of love"), he has warmed Sarah up toward himself and steals a
kiss, which soon advances to exchanging some kisses. "Oh my God,"
Sarah says, "What am I doing. . . ." Norman, the pragmatist, replies, kissing her all over, "I know what you're doing. Don't worry.
I'll tell you later." Immediately following, as another indication of
his charms, Annie invites Norman to her room "tonight" to make up
for the aborted weekend. Apparently, the Norman conquests have no end.

The final act is a clear series of conversations between various principals, serving in the best farcical way, to shed additional light on
the collection of motives, events, and consequences that essentially
make up the entire trilogy. Ruth, for example, has a revealing talk
with Tom, trying vainly to straighten him out on a few realities
about Norman and Annie. It is hard going since Tom's characteristic
responses are slow in coming—and usually incorrect. Near desperation as her attempts keep failing, Ruth believes she sees the problem.
"I think your brain works all right. I think what must happen is, it
receives a message from outside—but once that message gets inside
your head, it must be like an unfiled internal memo in a vast civil

service department. It gets shunted from desk to desk with nobody willing to take responsibility for it." The critical response was unanimous in heaping deserved praise on the plays. It was no hyperbole for the *Daily Mail* to say that "The three interlinked plays have carved a place in the history of British light comedy as indelible as 1066 itself."⁶ And J. W. Lambert in the *Sunday Times* hailed a brilliant comic achievement: "these plays . . . have an organic inner power, a truly classical grip. Structure and invention serve observation and understanding. What has long seemed likely is now clear: Mr. Ayckbourn, the Kingsley Amis of the stage, is the most remarkable British dramatist to have emerged since Harold Pinter."⁷ It was no surprise that the play won both the *London Evening Standard* and *Plays and Players* drama awards as the best of the year.

Chapter Seven
Absent Friends and *Confusions*

Absent Friends (1975)

In England "Absent Friends" is a common drinking toast; and here, in a cleverly arranged tea party, milder toasts serve up some of Ayckbourn's wickedest comedy, as good (?) friends gather to offer condolences to one of theirs who will need none. *Absent Friends* will draw a wide divergence of opinion.[1] One critic called it "woefully limp" with a weak story line and unintentional characters.[2] Another was ecstatic: "It's Mr. Ayckbourn's finest play, and if it is the saddest and most moving thing that he has written, it is also the most clear-sighted and the funniest."[3] The premise is a familiar one: Colin, the heralded guest, brings advice (and confusion) into the lives of the assembled. Here we have echoes of Hickey in O'Neill's *The Iceman Cometh* (1946) and Sir Henry Harcourt-Reilly in Eliot's *The Cocktail Party* (1950).

The opening scene introduces Evelyn and Diana, two strikingly singular and completely opposite women. Evelyn is a masterwork of comic invention—"a heavily made-up, reasonably trendily dressed expressionless girl" who evidently sees life on a cold, usually hostile footing. She chews gum constantly. Diana, older, thirties, equally experienced in the pains of life, is, nevertheless, gracious and perceptive. Whereas Diana *suggests* the tragic in her brave attempts to understand her life, Evelyn is bluntly what she is and never anything more. The differences quickly appear as Diana expresses concern about Evelyn's baby in the carriage.

> DIANA.   Should he be covered up as much as that, dear?
>
> EVELYN.   Yes.
>
> DIANA.   Won't he get too hot?
>
> EVELYN.   He likes it hot.
>
> DIANA.   Oh, I was just worried he wasn't getting enough air.
>
> EVELYN.   He's all right. He doesn't need much air.

Diana is hosting an afternoon tea to welcome an old friend, Colin, who lost his fiancée two months ago. They both await their husbands; however, as Diana goes on to some extent about her difficult life with Paul, Evelyn remains completely indifferent. Whenever some rejoinder is expected from Evelyn, the result is usually either an "Oh" or a simple "No."

Marge arrives, having left her husband, Gordon, ill at home. After Evelyn leaves the room, Diana confides to Marge her suspicions about Evelyn and the untrusting Paul. She believes that they are having an affair, admits she even tried to get Evelyn to say something, and seems convinced she is the one—"I've never trusted her an inch. She's got one of those really mean little faces, hasn't she?" We learn more background information about old friends, Paul and Colin, and how inseparable they were until Colin went off to a new job and to marry. All the while this is going forward, Evelyn is busily reading a magazine article on how to keep "the man in your life" happy. They make the error of asking Evelyn what she is reading, and Evelyn begins to recite excerpts in a flat monotone, continuing on even when they have had enough. Nevertheless, the somber advice rolls out: "Twelve tips by a woman psychiatrist. . . . Tip number one; send him off in the morning with a smile. . . . Make yourself into his news of the day . . . pamper yourself with a full beauty treatment. . . ." Finally, after a number of ineffectual "Yes, thank you Evelyn," pleas from Diana, Evelyn comes to an abrupt halt with her own critique: "I'm not doing that for my bloody husband. He can stuff it."

Paul comes home, has had words with Diana about Colin—not anxious to see him—and disappears upstairs. Alone with Evelyn, Marge forces the issue and asks her if it is true about Paul and her:

MARGE.   Have you been . . . having . . . a love affair with Paul?

EVELYN.   No.

MARGE.   Truthfully?

EVELYN.   I said no.

MARGE.   Oh. Well. That's all right then. [*Pause*]

EVELYN.   We did it in the back of his car the other afternoon but I wouldn't call that a love affair.

MARGE.   You and Paul did?

EVELYN.   Yes.

MARGE.   How digusting.

EVELYN.   It wasn't very nice.

The double meanings continue, as Evelyn goes on to say what she means by "very nice." It is the quality of the rumble she comments on and not the social stigma: "I'm not likely to do it again. He'd just been playing squash. He was horrible." And she continues, as Marge shows astonishment, to repeat the word "horrible" for Paul's performance and a number of other husbands she has sampled. "They all think they're experts with women. None of them are usually. And by the time they are, most of them aren't up to it anymore." And, finally, to cap it off, Evelyn informs the shocked Marge that John knows about the two of them but allows it since he needs Paul for his business. The network into which Colin will soon enter begins to tighten.

While we await Colin's arrival, we also have a chance to meet John, a "jiggling, restless figure," always on the lookout for bargains and quick deals. His continual dancing movements bother the others as well; Evelyn says he dances around the table at meals. He, too, is awkward about seeing Colin again. What will they talk about? He certainly does not want to hear about Colin's fiancée's death—"I hate death. Gives me the creeps." We also have time to learn more about their earlier time together with Colin. Diana, deliberately tense with Paul, reminds him that Colin used to date her sister, Barbara. And why did Paul not have an affair with her? The mood between them gets more ugly as more recriminations fly about. Finally, Diana accuses the two of them—Paul and Evelyn—openly. Paul vehemently denies it. Their heated argument neatly overlaps Marge's telephone conversation with Gordon, who has just spilled his cough mixture:

DIANA.   You know bloody well what I'm talking about. I'm talking about you and her, you bastard.

MARGE.   Has it sunk through to the mattress, love?

The device may be an old one, and we have seen it before in Ayckbourn; but used here, it seems to be a master stroke of comic balance. It is masterful because we are thus able, so easily, to have that wonderful blending of the serious and the trifling. And it is with this mixture of excited voices that the doorbell finally—thankfully—introduces Colin to the play.

The unmournful mourner. From the moment they greet him at the door, everyone is shocked to find that Colin is not the broken and distressed man they expected; instead he is a glowingly joyous glad-hander. He fairly bounces with radiant energy, surveying them all "from the height of an impregnable joy."[4] All of the friends' attempts to avoid the subject of death are quickly sidetracked when they realize how anxious Colin is to talk about Carol. "But the irony is that not only does Colin turn out to be unstoppably loquacious about the dead girl but that he is also an agent of disaster who cheerily exposes the running marital sores, the private angers, and frustrations of everyone in the room."[5] It will not take very long, as the tea party progresses, for a beautiful love-hate relationship to be established between Colin and his friends, very much like the position of Hickey in *The Iceman Cometh,* who has come to "rescue" his derelict bar buddies.

Colin even insists on showing them photos of the good times he had with Carol. Ultimately, he launches into the longest speech of the act:

And I suppose when I first met Carol, it must have passed through my mind what would I feel like if I did lose her. . . . and then it happened. . . . She was caught in this under-current. . . . And for about three weeks after that, I couldn't do anything at all. Nothing. I just lay about thinking, remembering and then, all of a sudden, it came to me that if my life ended there and then, by God, I'd have a lot to be grateful for. I mean, first of all, I'd been lucky enough to have known her. I don't know if you've ever met a perfect person. But that's what she was. The only way to describe her. And I, me, I'd had the love of a perfect person. And that's something I can always be grateful for.

But then, he continued, pointing to the people in the room, all his life he had good friends, real people, and he named them all in turn. "I'm not bitter about what happened. Because I've been denied my own happiness, I don't envy or begrudge you yours. I just want you to know that despite everything that happened, in a funny sort of way, I too am happy." The effect on the others is disastrous; this is not at all what they had been led to expect, especially in their bumbling attempts to avoid the word—"death." Here was the bereaved "looking around at them serenely." Diana weeps hysterically and rushes out; Marge blows her nose loudly; John, who had earlier begun his jiggling about, looks sickly, and gives Colin a ghastly smile;

Paul opens his mouth but nothing comes out—and Evelyn, expressionless, continues her gum chewing!

Act 2 continues the general air of forced pleasantries. More talk follows about the past, the good old days. Conversation turns in a number of directions; and then Colin, genial as ever, admits that he has the knack of sizing people up, of knowing their problems. He has not met Evelyn before, but somehow, as he stares intently at her, he has a feeling that something is bothering her. The indifferent Evelyn simply answers, "Right." Colin warms quickly to the challenge: "There you are. Now I'm going to go a bit further and I warn you I'm going to stick my neck out now and say one of your worries is John. Right?" Evelyn's answer ("Amazing"), said in the same monotone, does not faze Colin a bit as he warms further to the full analysis. Here, obviously, is the science of positive thinking in full display.

It is another excellent comic effect to hear his advice to Evelyn, which sorely lacks the knowledge we already have of the real issues. Colin says that John is an extrovert and his wife may be in his shadow. "My advice is," he tells Evelyn, "don't let your personality— because I can see there is a lovely personality hiding under there— don't let that get buried away. Because he won't thank you for it in the end. Nobody will. Get in the habit of giving yourself to people, if you know what I mean and you'll get a lot more back, believe me. I'm a giver. . . ." These are astonishing, ironic remarks when we recall that Evelyn has been "giving herself to people" quite generously, having slept with most of the available married men, including Diana's Paul. As may be expected, the only answer to Colin's analysis is an overwhelming silence.

Memoir time. Talk drifts back again to the past; Colin is anxious to dredge up old stories about the old gang. The mixed reception to "memoir time" is amusing; Paul would rather *not* hear; Diana, fishing for clues to their existence, does; Marge, the social moderator, merely wants to placate Colin. As the story begins, Paul, who is restless and nervous, objects, "Look, this was a long time ago." Colin explains that that is the reason for telling it. Diana has one quick word for her mate, "Shut up." The story is an awkward one for Paul since it tells how in their courting days he had come to tea at Diana's and had broken some china ducks on the wall. Later, he had repaired them and returned them to the wall, and no one ever knew. At the end of the tea, Paul took Diana's napkin home, an act which Colin judged to be romantic. At first, Paul said it was untrue, and then he remembered that he still had the napkin. "Yes, I use it to clean the car with." Diana's reaction is swift and direct; she picks up the cream jug and slowly pours it over Paul's head. Paul is indignant and cannot believe it; Diana is nonchalant about it ("accidents will happen") and turns casually back to her role as tea hostess, "now then, tea for you, John?"

Colin, ever ready, jumps into the breach and gives a defense for Paul, saying that at heart he is a romantic but that he has covered it up. And this is how Paul has made a success of his life. We should, Colin concludes, "love him for what he is." Diana, in a trance of her own, very quietly begins a moving monologue, perhaps the highpoint of the entire play. First, she talks of a red coat which she always wanted when she was a girl and finally got—but then it did not look right—"Because I had this burning ambition you see, to join the Canadian Royal Mounted Police."

MARGE. Good gracious. . . .

DIANA. People used to say "You can't join the Mounted Police. You're a little girl. Little girls don't join the Mounted Police. Little girls do nice things like typing and knitting and nursing and having babies." So I married Paul instead. Because they refused to let me join the Mounted Police. I married him because he kept asking me. And because people kept saying that it would be a much nicer thing to do than . . . and so I did. And I learnt my typing and I had my babies and I looked after them for so long as they'd let me and then suddenly I realized I'd been doing all the wrong things. They'd been wrong telling me to marry Paul and have babies, if they're not even going to let you keep them, and I should have joined the Mounted Police, that's what I should have done. I know I should have joined the Mounted Police. [Starting to sob] I want to join the Mounted Police. Please. . . .

The sobs become louder and louder till they become a series of short staccato screams. Everyone is stunned; Paul comes down to help Diana but she fights him away. Finally, they lead her out. The play soon comes to an adequate close, with a few more comic diversions. Colin continues to make inappropriate judgments of character, Marge works her soothing powers, and John gives a fully hilarious defense of his life with Evelyn; "The good thing about Evelyn . . . is that she has absolutely no sense of humour . . . you never have to waste your time trying to cheer her up. Misery is her natural state." And in Marge's final farewell (at the door) to Colin, she misses the mark again and says we should get together again, "once you've got over . . . I mean, I know it will be difficult . . . for you to forget about Carol. . . ."

Ayckbourn confided that when *Absent Friends* is compared to a sure winner such as *The Norman Conquests,* it needed his special care: "I have soft spots for certain ones, but that may just be because they are not able to take care of themselves." He was aware in the writing that it would not appeal to everyone. "I deliberately laid down all the safe apparatus one uses to ensure that something works." He admits that he can now safely write laughable scenes very easily, but in this play he left out the usual, sometimes mechanical mixture. "It's like fighting," he explains, "and saying, 'I'm not going to use my right hook because I know it's very strong, I'll use my left.' It sounds as if I deliberately tried to write a bad play which wasn't actually true. I tried to write something different. . . ."6 The difference meant, as he explains, that he went *"round* all the jokes, deliberately stopping at points where, perhaps, one could have broadened into more obvious farce. I was trying to do something much more low key."7

Confusions (1976)

Confusions is billed as "An Entertainment," and that it certainly is.8 Ayckbourn has cleverly grouped five one-act plays (somewhat linked together) into both comic and satiric displays in his continuing saga of life in the English suburbs. It is true, perhaps, that "separation," "obsession," or "isolation" may be more accurate generic titles for the five playlets, but the essential theme still remains—that we fail most amusingly (and sadly) in our attempts to communicate. The device of linking these short pieces together, by having one character going on into the succeeding play, works to some extent. However, after awhile it fails to matter, except in the first two plays where there is a statement worth making between the actions of the two plays. Since the first play, by indirection, concerns an absent husband, it follows to have the husband, next, demonstrate what he does in his absence—pursuing two females in an out-of-town pub.

"Mother Figure"—most aptly titled—concerns the spouse of the above, who is completely mired down in the mind-deadening tasks of caring for three demanding little children. For a number of weeks, with hubby gone on the road, she has been in complete isolation with her charges, continually calling after them ("Nicholas! Stay in your own bed and leave Sarah alone") to the extent that she is literally lost to the outside world. Sad events, but in Ayckbourn's masterful handling the results may well be one of the most successful comic pieces the playwright has done—successful even more so, I would suggest, because of the extreme economy with which everything is accomplished. Lucy, the mother, is thoroughly convincing to us as she runs back and forth, trying to control the children. Abruptly, a neighbor, Rosemary, comes to the door, inquiring about Lucy's welfare since no one has seen her in weeks. More to the point, she is doing a particular service since the errant husband, Harry, telephoned her to try to contact his wife. We have already seen that Lucy has the habit of not answering the phone.

In short order we find Lucy ordering her neighbor around with the same tone as if she were addressing the children. And, most remarkably, the mild-mannered Rosemary falls right into the role. When the guest drinks the proffered orange juice, Lucy counsels her sharply—and gets the suitable response.

> LUCY.   Rosemary dear, try not to make all that noise when you drink.
>
> ROSEMARY. Sorry.

When Rosemary's husband, Terry, arrives to retrieve her, he soon falls into the same "mother-child" relationship. The couple have an argument and Lucy calms them, even to the extent of waving a doll ("Mr. Poodle's watching you") in Rosemary's face—all remarkable stage business but thoroughly convincing—and very funny! The play ends with a darkened stage and a single spot on Harry in a phone booth, still vainly trying to call home.

"Drinking Companion" gives us that other side of the story, the "adventure" of Harry at the out-of-town pub. The contrast is appropriate after the startling, novel effects of the earlier play. However, the material is much weaker. The problem of the smooth-talking salesman getting nowhere with two glacierlike young girls has a limited potential. The idiom is convincing, nevertheless, in the high gear, self-promotional way Harry talks: "Bernice. Pretty name. Paula and Bernice—lovely names—and I thought to myself, hallo they don't belong here. They look right out of place. Two lovely personalities like yours just don't go together with Mason's. No. I thought to myself—they're from London I wouldn't mind betting." Drinks follow drinks, and suggestions for a closer encounter ("in room, two-four-nine"), but nothing avails. And we finally leave Harry waiting while the girls escape out a back way.

Two tables for two. "Between Mouthfuls" has far better possibilities with the opportunity for Ayckbourn to demonstrate his skilled way in moving fast-paced comic actions about. The arrangement is quite simple; two tables for two in a restaurant, out of sight of each other, being dutifully serviced by a waiter. The trick here is that one table holds the boss and his wife, the Pearces; and the other, the employee, Martin, and his wife, Polly. We overhear conversation only when the waiter is at that particular table. And with proper, careful timing, the waiter's inquiries will fit very amusingly into two heated arguments.

> PEARCE. Would you mind lowering your voice.
>
> MRS. PEARCE. I will not lower my voice.
>
> WAITER. Runner beans, madam?
>
> MRS. PEARCE. No thank you.
>
> WAITER. Carrots, madam?
>
> MRS. PEARCE. No, thank you. I want nothing else.
>
> WAITER. No potatoes either, madam?
>
> MRS. PEARCE. [*Shrilly*] Nothing else.

The Pearce argument concerns Mr. Pearce's recent business trip to Italy and the wife's conviction that there was another woman involved. The younger couple's argument concerns the husband's general neglect of his wife—a rather familiar Ayckbourn predicament. Polly was forced to take a holiday without Martin since he could not get away—a fact she sincerely doubts. "That's what it boils down to," she concludes, "I'm not in the slightest bit interested in your work and you don't give a damn what I'm up to. There we are. We haven't one thing in common." And then, to prove her point, Polly blurts out the awful truth that she spent "three weeks with Donald Pearce in a hotel in Rome." Martin's reaction gives us the theme of the play: his only concern is that he will lose his job when Mrs.

Pearce finds out. Polly is astounded that she still cannot get the right attention from her husband—and storms out. Mrs. Pearce follows suit and also leaves in a huff—after first flipping his plate into his lap. "I'm unable to enjoy a meal with a man who turns out to be a deceitful, lecherous liar."

"Gosforth's Fête" is a first-class farce with enough mechanicals going wrong to throw every one into a dither. Again, Ayckbourn proves himself the master of the form. Coincidences, embarrassments, a muddy rainstorm, alcoholic nondrinkers, running-free cub scouts— all combine to make the fund-raising event for a new community hall a complete disaster. "No playwright since Coward," Herbert Kretzmer shrewdly observes, "has the gift of catching this island race with its deferences and sometimes its pants down."[9] Fresh from the last play, Councilor Mrs. Pearce arrives at the tea tent as the guest of honor (and speaker) for the day's events. Everything is in a turmoil, as we might expect, with preparations going amiss; and all under the guiding and hammy hand of Gordon Gosforth, a beery-faced doubtful "leader of men" and present pub-keeper.

The most immediate task, as he informs Mrs. Pearce, is to have the loud speaker system operate properly. He gives her the run down on the day's schedule—if the tent ever goes up ("half the guy ropes are missing")—including the time for her speech, the four o'clock tea, the novelty races ("all that sort of rubbish"), and finally concluding at six o'clock. "All pack up, dismantle tents—seven-thirty all cleared away because old Swales wants the field back for his cows first thing in the morning." The continued rumble of thunder that goes on during the long recital gives us some idea of the adjustments that will have to be made. Number One Assistant is fresh-faced Milly Carter, more than just the tea lady as we abruptly find out. While Gosforth fiddles with the mike, Milly finally gets his attention ("it's frightfully urgent") and tells him that she is pregnant with his child.

Outspoken privacies. Gosforth drops the mike and the jolt causes it to become alive. Quite cleverly, we become aware, as they do not, that their voices are being heard across the field. (The trick is accomplished by having a series of loudspeakers echo their voices around the stage.) We learn, in their frantic conversation (as everyone now does) that this creates a problem with her fiancé, Stewart Stokes, the cub scout leader. Before anything can be resolved, the angry Stewart bursts into the scene, having heard everything over the loudspeakers.

STEWART. You bastard, Gosforth. . . .

GOSFORTH. Hallo, old boy.

STEWART. You complete and utter bastard, Gosforth.

GOSFORTH. Now keep calm, Stokes.

STEWART. I'm going to kill you, Gosforth.

GOSFORTH. Stokes, keep calm.

STEWART. With my bare hands. . . . How do you think it feels to hear the news that my fiancée is pregnant by another man? Isn't that bad enough? But when you publicly announce it over four acres of field . . . in front of all my Cubs. . . .

GOSFORTH. I say, Stewart, I'm sorry.

STEWART. There are Brownies out there as well you know.

Appearances, as in all of life, become more important than reality, and they finally manage to quiet Stewart down with a supply of sherry, something the resolute Stewart usually never touches—and this alone is another trick. However, our wronged citizen manages to "cooperate" after awhile, using the ready bottle to punctuate a number of pungent epithets ("you fascist"—"you swine") as he sits and broods over the uncertain future. Appropriate to the farce form, a number of quick events move the tempo along. The rains come, and even more frantic running about. The cub scouts throw mud at each other. A decision is made to have an early tea—and speech. Mrs. Pearce appears in a sad, limp condition, shoes and stockings coated in mud. It seems that she was misdirected by the cub scouts and "finished up in a ploughed field."

Mrs. Pearce somehow manages to give her talk. While she delivers a frankly inappropriate political speech, a frantic bit of stage business begins to divert everyone. Milly turns on the tap of the tea urn for a cup of tea and is unable to turn it off. In swift succession, the tea "committee" runs about, filling up every cup in sight. They had started with three hundred and fifty cups. More mayhem takes place before, gratefully, the farce comes to an end. The essence of good farce, we are reminded by Michael Billington, is "a matter of rearranging the furniture on the Titanic."[10]

The final play, "A Talk in the Park," is a Brechtian series of monologues delivered in turn by five occupants of park benches. Arthur, "a bird-like man in a long mackintosh," rattles on about the superi-

ority of women. They are better, cleaner, with kinder hearts; and if
he could choose, he would be one. "When I choose to have a conversation, I can tell you it's with a woman everytime. Because a woman
is one of nature's listeners. Most men I wouldn't give the time of day
to. . . . Trouble is, I don't get to meet as many women as I'd like
to." The others half listen; and at the end of each delivery, someone,
properly restless with what he hears, moves on to another bench.
Beryl, an angry young girl, wants to be left alone to read a long letter. She, in turn, talks at length, violently, against violence. We hear
an account of a former boyfriend ("a right bastard") who has beaten
her up. "Sometimes I just want to jump down a deep hole and forget
it. Only I know that bastard'll be waiting at the bottom. Waiting to
thump the life out of me."

Charles, a businessman, has more problems than this playlet could
accommodate. Everything has gone wrong: his wife died suddenly,
his children emigrated to Canada, and he now lives in a miniscule
flat. Trouble, he tells us, is "a bit like woodworm"; it starts to spread
everywhere. "Which explains why I'm sitting here reading a report
that's been put together so badly that I've got to read it through on
my one day off and condense it into another report before I can even
be certain whether I'm bankrupt." Before he concludes, Doreen,
middle-aged and untidy, has heard enough and moves away. Her
general complaint is men—all men. She made a choice a while back
between her husband and the dog he did not like. Now he is the *ex*-
husband and she glories in her present life with Ginger-boy who "understands every word I say to him."

The final monologue is given by a younger man, Ernest, who
launches into a full, five-star complaint against wives—and the entire
domestic system: "I came out here to get away from my wife. . . .
That's why I'm in the park. Get away from the noise. You got kids?
Don't have kids. Take my tip, don't get married. Looks all right, but
believe me—nothings your own. You've paid for it all but nothing's
your own. Yap, yap, yap. Want, want, want. Never satisfied. . . .
Sunday mornings, it's a race to see who can get out first. Loser keeps
the baby."

Perhaps the final play is a bit too severe in pushing its message
along about our excessive self-absorptions, but it may be suitable to
round off an evening of excursions into the human dilemma, clever
excursions which, fortunately, are more amusing than sad. In the full

Chekhovian tradition, *all* the plays may be reminders that conversation is largely a matter of interrupted monologues.[11] The critical acclaim for the plays seemed widely general. It may well be that Ayckbourn solves the always knotty problem of how to end full-length plays by simply giving us a sequence of comic sketches that need no pretense of completion or final resolution.

Chapter Eight

Bedroom Farce and
Just Between Ourselves

Bedroom Farce (1977)

It was a notable event both for Ayckbourn and the National Theatre that *Bedroom Farce* marked the first anniversary (almost to the day) of England's prized new theater on the South Bank.[1] It was also to be co-director Peter Hall's first venture into modern comedy since taking over the reins of the National Theatre in 1973 from Laurence Olivier. The critics were not disappointed. Carefully limiting his scope, Ayckbourn fashioned an enjoyable evening in the theater, according to Bernard Levin. The happy result "is a joyous nothing that makes up for many bleak nights of pretentious somethings."[2] Of course, knowing his limitations has always been a prime indication of Ayckbourn's outstanding abilities as a theater craftsman. It is also amusing to note that in a play so beguilingly titled, there is no sex whatsoever; "adultery is not only avoided, but barely contemplated." The three bedroom sets that fit across the stage are "each occupied by a lawful pair trying to get some sleep. That they cannot is the fault of the fourth team, Trevor and Susannah, who are also married, but are the type rarely to be found at home in bed, or at home at all."[3]

The play was also warmly welcomed because it was a robust return to full comedy following the controversial *Absent Friends* of two years earlier. The arrangement of the action is as outwardly simple as the frank alignment of three bedrooms which greets the audience. Three couples, as indicated above, have a series of comic events with each other plus the wandering fourth—Trevor and Susannah—which are presented to us solely through our "bedroom" views of their lives. As Ayckbourn has done before, all else (the real action) is offstage. What we watch are the fitful consequences. This was also to be the first time that Ayckbourn would use the cross-cutting device— from bedroom to bedroom—to such a great extent. "Jumping the action," as Ayckbourn points out, "gives the play an added rhythm over and above what the dialogue normally provides."[4]

The first bedroom (left stage) is a large Victorian in need of redecoration, belonging to Ernest and Delia, both nearing sixty. The second bedroom is contemporary ("candlewicked divan"), belonging to a thirtyish couple, Malcolm and Kate. The third bedroom is furnished in a more trendy style, for the young moderns Nick and Jan. At the start of the play Ernest and Delia are readying themselves for an evening out, their wedding anniversary. They talk of their son, Trevor ("always a difficult boy"), and apparent problems in his marriage with Susannah, a rather complex, despairing young lady. Perhaps he should have married Jan instead. The action cross fades to the bedroom of Nick and Jan. Nick, a rising young executive, is groaning on the bed with a bad back. "Totally unfair. Why me?" he complains. "I mean, I'm the last person in the world who should be stuck in bed. . . . I'm a naturally active person, aren't I? Aren't I. I have to be on the go. I need to be on the go. I'm going to go mad lying here, you know."

Jan does what she can for Nick—arranging for business calls at home, and so forth—but she plans to go to Malcolm and Kate's party. She wants, particularly, to see her ex-lover, Trevor, and perhaps help him in the rumored problems with the difficult Susannah.

JAN.   It's just I heard that—well—there's some awful trouble between them. I mean that silly bitch Susannah, she's got no idea at all. She hasn't a clue about Trevor. I know Trevor's impossible sometimes but I think I do know him probably better than anyone. . . .

NICK. Oh yes, yes.

JAN.   I think if I talk to them before they do something they'll regret. . . .

NICK. Like her shooting him.

JAN.   Don't be silly.

NICK. Look, he's a very selfish, very spoilt, self-pitying, self-obsessed. . . .

JAN.   I know. I know.

NICK. All right.

JAN.   Just for ten minutes. I promise.

Despite Nick's continuing doubts about the entire business with Susannah and Trevor, he grudgingly lets Jan leave. The fact that Jan and Trevor were once lovers bothers him as much as his ailing back. He is convinced that his incapacity is more serious than Jan allows. "It is just a little tiny muscle," Jan says, preparing (finally) to leave. Not so, Nick wails: "It is the main motor muscle that runs right up the spinal cord. . . ." Finally, with the reminder that it is only him—no one else—whom she loves, she leaves.

Cross fade now to the bedroom of Malcolm and Kate, probably the most outwardly comic pair of the evening. They are both jesters of the first order, continually playing tricks on each other—hiding shoes in the bed, spraying shaving soap on each other. There seems to be no end to their tricks as they try to get dressed for their house warming party. Invariably, they call truces—and instantly break them. For example, Kate finally recovers her lost shoe in the bed ("Oh really"), cries out "no more"—and then stuffs Malcolm's boots into one of the pillow cases. The entire business after awhile seems to be a matter of going ahead one and back two; they make very little progress in getting dressed. As a result, when the guests begin to arrive Kate is still wearing only a towel and still pursuing the elusive Malcolm with her aerosol can in the ready position. She is forced to jump back into the bed as the first guests mount the stairs to deposit the coats in the bedroom per Malcolm's instructions.

Trevor's troubles.   The arrival of the distracted, self-obsessed Trevor in the room with a coat to deposit and the position of Kate under the covers adds up to first-class farce material. Ayckbourn makes the most of it. Again, innate British politeness furthers the ridiculous conversation:

KATE.   Hallo Trevor.

TREVOR.   Oh, hallo there.

KATE.   Hallo.

TREVOR.   Are you ill?

KATE.   No.

TREVOR.   Ah.

KATE.   I'm just getting changed.

TREVOR.   Ah. Er—Malcolm said it would be all right to put my coat on the bed. Is that O.K. with you?

KATE.   Fine.

TREVOR.   Won't make you too hot, will it?

KATE.   Uh?

TREVOR.   I mean with all the coats on top of you. Could get a bit hot by the middle of the evening.

KATE.   Oh no. I'm not staying here. I'm just . . . resting.

TREVOR.   Oh, great.

Undismayed, Trevor launches into casual conversation about Susannah who will be arriving shortly. At the moment, Malcolm arrives with Trevor's drink, takes in the scene and is confused: "Oh."

KATE.   Hallo.

MALCOLM. What are you doing?

KATE.   Nothing.

MALCOLM. Oh, Right. [*Handing Trevor his drink*] Here you are then.

Again polite conversation ensues, this time the three of them, on the subject of the apartment and Susannah.

Trevor, who characterically sees only half of what is in front of him, is deep within his own disturbed self, mumbling a number of semiincoherent phrases of the process: "Susannah and I have committed ourselves to . . . a totally outgoing—non-egotistical—givingness . . . a total submerging, you know." In addition, he has a habit of delaying the completion of his sentences; his voice tails off in its earnest groping while the others politely wait. No one waits more "politely" than the frantic Kate under the covers. She finally gets a pile of her clothes from Malcolm and dives under the covers to dress while Trevor drones on and on—and more guests can be heard mounting the steps with their coats.

A number of times during the above scene we cross fade to the two other bedrooms. Whenever we "visit" Nick we find him in an increasingly comic predicament due to his immobility on the bed. He has dropped his book, and he follows a series of frustrating movements ("Why me? Why me?") in failing to retrieve it. When we "look in" on Ernest and Delia, they are still preparing to leave. Ernest is periodically checking the attic for a water leak and messing up his evening wear. Another later look shows them returning from the restaurant and displeased with the meal. Too expensive compared to last year ("and that asparagus was out of a tin"), plus the disconcerting fact that no one was dressed properly. No ties, and design labels "all over their bottoms." In her day, Delia recalls, "I spent all my time making sure nobody could read my labels." They decide to cap the evening in an old, familiar way—"sardines on toast in bed." Back with Kate and her problems, we find her meeting Susannah— and her coat—in the bedroom. Susannah, a virtual demon of despair, was in true form when Malcolm let her in. "She burst into tears," Malcolm reports, "and ran straight into the bathroom." Her scene with Kate is another involvement with a self-obsessed problem child. With riveting intensity, Susannah tries to explain herself to Kate who is trying to complete her dressing under the covers. Susannah questions her about her love life with Malcolm ("Is it still exciting?") while Kate tries to evade a direct answer. Evidently, the fire has gone out between Susannah and Trevor:

SUSANNAH.   God, Trevor used to excite me. I was so excited by that
            man. Do you know what it feels like to be really excited?
KATE.   Yes. Yes. I think so.
SUSANNAH.   When we weren't actually physically here in the bed
            . . . you know, making love—I felt empty—utterly
            incomplete.
KATE.   Yes, it's nice sometimes, isn't it. . . .
SUSANNAH.   And now. Now, it's a desert. We hardly touch, you
            know.
KATE.   Oh.
SUSANNAH.   I think I actually revolt him.
KATE.   Oh, surely not.
SUSANNAH.   I sometimes feel that. Suddenly I've lost all my
            identity. . . .

Kate has managed to complete her dressing under the covers, and finally leaves to welcome the guests downstairs. Susannah asks to lie down awhile ("pluck up courage")—and throws herself dramatically back on the pillow. Her head strikes something. Boots in the pillow case. Another marital puzzlement for the bewildered Susannah.

However, direct confrontations in the person of Trevor arrive almost immediately at the bedroom door. Kate ushers him in ("Here he is, Susannah. Found him for you") and wisely, quickly, leaves. A major comic scene follows in a heated review of the couple's many problems. Susannah accuses the muddled Trevor of being coarse and violent; he rebuts by saying she made him violent—"I was a pacifist before I met you."

SUSANNAH. I wish I'd listened to that man.

TREVOR. What man?

SUSANNAH. That man we consulted just before we were married. The one who did the palm readings.

TREVOR. What, him?

SUSANNAH. He told me you were potentially a violent person. He was absolutely right. You've broken all my things. All my things I brought from home. All my china animals.

TREVOR. I told you, I'm sorry. I'll buy you some more.

SUSANNAH. I don't want some more. I wanted those.

TREVOR. I didn't mean to break them.

SUSANNAH. Then why did you throw a chair at them if you didn't mean to break them?

TREVOR. I don't know. I just felt like throwing a chair, that's all. No law against throwing chairs is there? It was my chair.

SUSANNAH. Potentially violent. That's what he said. That man.

TREVOR. He was an idiot.

SUSANNAH. No, he wasn't. My mother always went to him.

The argument is a marvelous example of Ayckbourn's ability with nonsequiturs. The defense for throwing a chair is simply, "It was *my* chair." Logic and anything remotely resembling common sense sail blithely out the window as their tempers rise. And the easy reliance on a "palm reader" for premarital counseling is an ingeniously clever stroke, which is made even more effective in Susannah's defense of his credentials—mother went to him! With little effort we get a hilarious mental picture of what the mother must be like. Eventually—predictably—the two come to blows, and go rolling off the bed. When Susannah threatens to throw a lamp at him, Trevor's characteristic defense is not to do it because "it's not yours."

In swift order a series of further farcical events give us the essential plot, which will be resolved in the next and final act. Malcolm separates the two; Susannah leaves; Jan comforts Trevor, an innocent kiss resulting, which the returning Susannah sees. Kate offers Trevor a back bedroom to spend the night, but he says he must first see Jan and Nick and explain the kiss. Thus, in rather arbitrary, mechanical ways—not unexpected in a farce—we have the situation set up for two very early morning visits to the two other bedrooms: Trevor to visit Jan and Nick, and Susannah to visit Ernest and Delia. And Kate and Malcolm will wait up for Trevor to return.

Nocturnal visits. In defense of the Ayckbourn method, Jack Kroll points out that "some have called his ingenious farces mechanical, but so is Newton's universe. Newton needed all his ingenuity to show how things work; Ayckbourn needs all his to show how things don't . . . Ayckbourn takes you to humanity's last refuge, the bed, and proves conclusively how impossible it has become to be peacefully or pleasurably horizontal."[5] There is also something mildly ironic in having these bed scenes for thrashing out problems of the human psyche. We are reminded of the professional analyst's ubiquitous couches, so much a part of our modern life. Here, of course, everything is wildly haphazard, and our principals find beds—and analyses, welcomed or not—wherever they can. As Anthony Curtis illustrates, there is an attempt here to find a balance between "supportive" and "destructive" people (as sociologists define them). "The problem is to provide the latter with the help they so desperately require without yourself becoming destroyed in the process."[6]

Act 2 has the lights up on all three areas. Action and dialogue jump from one area to another without formal interruption. The effect produces an excellent farcical pace. Since they must stay up to let Trevor in, Malcolm and Kate opt for the "constructive"; she watches avidly as would-be handyman Malcolm tries to put together a dressing table from a kit. "Only take me fifteen minutes," Malcolm announces, as he hauls out a number of cardboard boxes. With his tools spread around, Malcolm tackles his manly task while Kate starts an earnest discussion on their sex life. Taking off from comments about Trevor and Susannah's problems, she asks him if she still excites him. Malcolm answers too quickly, absentmindedly, "Oh yes. Mad about you. . . . Where the hell is locking bar C?"

> KATE.   I'd hate you to get bored.
>
> MALCOLM. I'm not bored. I'm just trying to find locking bar C.
>
> KATE.   You will tell me if you get bored with me, won't you?

MALCOLM. Yes, sure sure.

KATE. And I promise to tell you.

At the bedroom of Ernest and Delia they patiently await the appearance of Susannah, who has entered below. As usual, she has gone straight to the bathroom in tears. Finally, Susannah enters and tells her woeful tale to her in-laws: Trevor "deliberately making love to another woman." Delia defends Jan whom she knows well, and calls it all nonsense. But Susannah is convinced that her husband has lost his sexual interest in her—the "problem of the bed" as Delia puts it. The generation gap between the two women looms immense as Delia gives her solution: "Oh dear. Dear me. My mother used to say, 'Delia, if SEX ever rears its ugly head, close your eyes before you see the rest of it.' "

Trevor has arrived at the bedroom of Nick and Jan, at one in the morning, to explain the compromising kiss. To the sleepy Nick it will be a long, drawn out story: "it was nothing at all . . . nothing to it at all . . . but I wanted you to be the first to know about it." When Jan returns with tea she finds Trevor asleep on the chair. He awakes abruptly, half into an unfinished sentence of apology. Nick would rather try to sleep—his spine is still a problem—but Trevor insists on discussing Susannah. Eventually, they allow Trevor to spend the night on the couch. But first he calls Kate and tells them not to wait up. A quick shift—it is now 3:00 A.M.—to Malcolm and Kate, and we find a completely frustrated Malcolm breaking parts, determined somehow to put the kit together. At the bedroom of Ernest and Delia they have made arrangements for Susannah to spend the night with Delia, while Ernest is relegated to the spare room.

Finally, Malcolm finishes the table, but he admits—as we can see—that certain modifications had to be made since it stands lopsided and ridiculous. Delia spends a fitful night with Susannah, who suffers from nightmares and makes weird, moaning sounds—and finally claws and clutches at Delia. At 6:45 Susannah insists that she must telephone Trevor. No answer at their home; Susannah wants to try Malcolm's. Delia warns her that "you're going to be dreadfully unpopular" at this hour. What now follows will be a series of strictly farcical phone calls, fully guaranteed to get rolls of audience laughter. Basically preposterous at this early hour, the very idea strikes a universal chord for the absurd in life. Susannah calls Delia who tells her that Trevor is spending the night at Jan's. That news sends Susannah off into another paroxysm of tears and cries, which awakens Ernest in the next room. Delia persuades Ernest to ring Jan; and after much confusion, the parted young lovers, Trevor and Susannah, talk to each other. They agree to meet, despite the hour, at Malcolm's house, since Trevor owes *them* an apology. At Malcolm's, Kate lets Trevor in since Malcolm has fallen asleep with his clothes on next to the dressing table. Trevor examines the table, which Kate shows off as Malcolm's great nocturnal accomplishment. He tries to straighten it out and the entire table collapses. The play relievedly comes to a close with the two young lovers, reconciled, resting on the bed. They slip under the covers and are surprised to find sauce pans and boots for company.

The great popularity of *Bedroom Farce* must always be the first consideration in any assessment of its place in contemporary theater. Together with *Absurd Person Singular,* these two plays have had the longest runs of all the Ayckbourn plays. Each ran for two years and four months, with *Bedroom Farce* doing another eight months in New York, and *Absurd Person Singular* adding two more years in New York. Such wide appeal must speak for itself despite the critical reservations which are always present. Good farce (as all good theater) *succeeds on the stage alone,* no matter what sober reevaluations follow the next morning. And it seems imperative to keep in mind that, more so in comedy than in straight drama, theatricality must win out over analysis. We never know entirely why we are convulsed with laughter during the evening; we only know that somehow the elements have been rightly present to work their effects on us. And this is even more true with farce, which by nature of its definition turns reason and good sense around and catches us fully unaware.

Bedroom Farce received a good press in both London and New York, and deserves its high regard because it is completely satisfying as a good evening's fun. To what extent Ayckbourn's success is due to a practiced formula is incidental to the fact that the method usually works well enough. As the title indicates, there were no other, more subtle obligations that Ayckbourn had to adhere to.

Just Between Ourselves (1977)

Although *Absent Friends* (1975) had earlier given clear indications that the immensely successful *comic* Ayckbourn had a major serious side as well, the 1977 production of *Just Between Ourselves* was a so-

bering surprise to critics and audience alike.[7] Here for the first time
in the lengthening Ayckbourn canon was a view of middle-class English life which managed to have as many serious considerations as
humorous ones. According to Irving Wardle in his next-day review,
there are two Ayckbourns in contrast here: "the master comic tech-
nician" and "the bleak anatomist of the marriage trap." And "for
every belly-laugh . . . there are 10 times when you crack a smile of
rueful recognition."[8] Michael Billington is even more to the point
when he says that the low-toned play has "the kick of an angry
mule."[9]

The best way, however, to appraise the plays of this period is to
use Ayckbourn's own term: he calls this "the first of my 'winter'
plays."[10] And he means it literally as well since he had begun to write
plays for his Scarborough theater on a year-round basis, now for the
first time writing in December for January performances. Before, he
had always, in his boiler-work manner, written in late spring for the
Scarborough summer season. Ayckbourn gives us an excellent picture
of himself in his converted vicarage doing battle with the elements—
and his muse: "As is customary, I wrote mainly at night—but this
was my first experience of tackling a play whilst the North Sea storms
hurtled round the house, slates cascading from the roof and metal
chimney cowlings were bouncing off parked cars below my window,
rebounding hither and thither like demented pinballs. Not surprisingly, the result was a rather sad (some say a rather savage) play."[11]

Even a modest probing of essential character can be devastating
when the usual ordinary, calming—and often humorous—props are
suddenly removed. For most of the earlier plays, Ayckbourn has been
dealing (and with great success) with the everyday props of reality.
"As one grows courage as a playwright," Ayckbourn says, "one takes
time to stop and scrape more layers off the characters: and as you take
away these layers, you get into all sorts of bones and awfulness which
are normally way below the surface, and which belong to desperate
people."[12] There seems no doubt that with this play, "the winter
play," Ayckbourn has turned a major corner in his career.

The action of the play takes place in the garage of Dennis and
Vera, a middle-aged couple. (By now unusual settings are no longer
surprising with Ayckbourn; he seems intent on demonstrating how
many different places in a house one can set a play.) We are, as always, in the English suburbia Ayckbourn knows so well. Dennis is
a well-meaning, jovial sort, with more confidence than proof in his

abilities as a handyman. Obviously, this will provide a number of turns of good comedy. As the play opens, he is wrestling with an electric kettle on the garage work bench. Vera introduces Neil, a prospect for the car they are trying to sell. In the ensuing conversation, enough quick remarks are made by Dennis to establish the important fact that he is a bit unthinking in his little jokes about Vera's occasional lapses. To a complete stranger, Dennis goes on about Vera "catching the kettle with her elbow." He adds—to Vera's embarrasment and Neil's confusion—that she catches everything with her elbow.

As Vera slips quietly away, all the attention is focused now on Dennis, the newcomer, Neil, and the car. In itself this entire scene is a good comic bit on "selling the family car." Along the way, however, we learn much of Dennis's characteristic ebullient nature; for example, his somewhat wild, premature ways of getting into people's lives. Quite abruptly, he becomes a lay-advisor to Neil's stomach problems. Every time Neil bends to examine the car he complains. "Oh dear," Dennis offers, "Been living it up, have you?" "No, No," Neil protests, "I only get it when I bend down." Nevertheless, Dennis launches out into a disquisition on personal health. Just as readily, he goes off on a number of tangents. He even gets greatly excited about astrological signs, an obvious passion in his life. How perfect, he exclaims, to the bewildered Neil, that Vera's sign, Pisces, corresponds so well with Neil's Scorpio! This is most meaningful since it is Vera's car that is being offered for sale. And Dennis becomes wildly ecstatic when he learns that Neil and his mother, Marjorie (who lives with them), have the same birthday.

A car for Pam. The befuddled Neil admits that the car is for his wife, Pam, who is in the house having tea with Vera and Marjorie, but apparently has no interest in viewing what is in the garage. Strange circumstance, but it does not stop the energetic Dennis, who suggests they "set the stage" with Neil casually at the wheel while Pam is ushered into the garage. Dennis, despite Neil's protestations that Pam does not react "that way," is convinced that it will work. The thoroughly comic scene that results (in the further stage of "selling the car") has a quiet disarming way of ending, which cleverly reveals some sober realities. After some heated exchanges between Neil and Pam on the real worth of the car, Neil reminds her that the car is for the times she goes out:

PAM. When am I going to get out occasionally?

NEIL. I just thought. . . .

PAM. Where the hell am I supposed to be going?

Scene 1 ends with an appropriate (and effective) demonstration of a key element in the plot—the question of Vera's awkwardness. Alone with his mother, Marjorie, Dennis discusses Vera's health. Marjorie insists that Vera needs close watching, but Dennis suggests that everyone needs to laugh more about these things, the way he does. The convenient device of a balky door to the garage "proves" that Marjorie may be right about Vera. Carrying a tray of tea things through the door, Vera slips and drops everything in an enormous clatter, which they all witness. The scene ends with the smug Marjorie saying, "There you are, Dennis, what did I say?"

February has moved on to May in the next scene, and the two couples are close friends by now. While the car stands somewhat demurely in the background (in the opened wall of the garage set), a tea table is being prepared by Neil and Pam on the garden side of the garage. The occasion is Dennis's birthday. In their talk of their home life, we learn of Pam's basic restlessness ("There's lots of things I want, Neil. But they're not to be, are they?") and of Neil's apparent helplessness. Later, Neil confesses to Dennis that he is confused by Pam, that she wakes him in the middle of the night—with passionate desires at 4:00 A.M.! Apparently, neither of the men seem to be able to put some obvious signs together and come up with a true reading of the real dangers in Pam's life. Here, of course, we have a central thread in the pattern of the entire play. The drama will reveal that both wives are in desperate emotional trouble, and the essential irony will be in Dennis's characteristic answer to all problems—the ready laugh—and in Neil's hesitant assertions.

A possible strained example of Neil's ineptness is found in his ready willingness to be led by newfound friend Dennis into a capital investment. Dennis convinces Neil ("just between ourselves") that he should back a decorator who is anxious to start his own business. Considering that the money is a one-time windfall from his father's will, we are a bit surprised that Neil moves so quickly to make what turns out (at the end of the play) to be such a foolish and costly move. The decorator, George Spooner, runs off with his secretary, and leaves the wife and the business greatly "in arrears." Characteristic of

Dennis when he hears this news is his astrological assessment: "He was a Capricorn . . . [they] just don't do that sort of thing. It's not in their nature." But nevertheless, this Capricorn does, and Neil is out a bundle.

A place for mother. The highpoint of the first act is toward the end where Ayckbourn stages another one of his mealtime comic disasters. (We are reminded, most notably, of *How the Other Half Loves* and *The Norman Conquests*.) Here, however, this being a "winter" play, there is an additional burden in the stage business; the scene must further the basic plot (Vera's breakdown) as well as roll us in the aisles. Here, perhaps, is the true test of Ayckbourn, the sober jester. The principals gather outside on this cool day in May to have their birthday tea for Dennis. The initial task is to place mother where there will be the least draft. Marjorie hesitantly comes out expecting the worst, all bundled up with a small blanket and a hot water bottle. The others keep moving Marjorie and the table and chairs about ("Which way's the wind"), at the same time hurriedly passing along the blanket and the hot water bottle and her handbag. Vera finally puts a halt to the circus when she appears with the tea things. She orders them to place Marjorie over to the side, some distance from the table—with her blanket, handbag, and hot water bottle. The others group themselves around the table.

While Marjorie continues to complain that Vera should have made a birthday cake for Dennis, Vera attempts to serve tea. The odds begin to mount against Vera keeping her stability: the cups begin to rattle more and more as she pours and passes. The others watch transfixed, waiting for the catastrophe. Finally, she spills everything! Dennis struggles to contain his laughter—and it finally erupts. His answer to everything hardly calms the distraught Vera; he softly sings "Happy Birthday to me" as the act ends.

Act 2 takes place in October and this time the occasion is the birthday of Neil and mother Marjorie. Neil and Dennis are in the garage conversing while Dennis power sands a needlework box he has made for his mother. Interesting comic effects follow as the drill nearly drowns out Neil's desperate remarks about his home problems. Nevertheless, Dennis keeps nodding his head. Meanwhile, in the house Pam stands buffer between the warring Vera and Marjorie, who refuse to talk to each other. Vera has to come to the garage to ask Dennis to ask his mother to lower the television. Dennis tells her to go in and be nice to her, say Happy Birthday, Mother, give her a little drink. "She doesn't need a little drink," Vera replies. "She's already downed half the bottle." He seems to have no idea how desperate things are with his wife. When Vera pleads for some help around the house—more of his presence *out* of the garage—he can only answer by saying that she should give him a list of things he should do for her around the house. A presentiment of worse things to come is evident in the slow, sad way Vera shuffles back into the conjugal home.

Dennis outlines to Neil his plan to surprise Marjorie: she will enter the garage, he will turn on the colored strung lights he has erected, uncover the present, while Neil follows behind her with the birthday cake. Everyone will sing Happy Birthday! Somehow, we are inclined to doubt Dennis's exalted prophecy of things to come: "And you just watch mother's face. It'll be a picture. A real study." Neil, of course, continues to wallow in his recounts of his unhappy home life.

Alone with Dennis in the garage, Pam has *her* turn to confess her equally unhappy state with Neil. Her depression nearly equals Vera's: she feels "old, unfulfilled, frustrated, unattractive, dull, washed out, undesirable—you name it"—and nothing ahead. Dennis responds with countenances of patience. Neil, he assures her, still wants her. Pam wants Dennis "to jolly me up" and she sits in the car, playfully making signs of a motor starting up ("Brrm, brrm"). The glass she has been holding is beginning to have an effect and, after another wild outburst ("Brrm, brrm"), she says that she is going to be car sick! Dennis-to-the-rescue turns into a complete farcical involvement with the woman, which action is, naturally, completely misread by Marjorie, and Vera in turn.

Marjorie walks in while Dennis and Pam are entangled with each other in the car seat and assumes thay are being "naughty." Vera's reaction is to turn hysterically on Marjorie, accusing her of enjoying this scene ("You poisonous old woman. You're loving this, aren't you?"), giving proof as it might to the mother's continual reminder to Vera of her failures as a wife. Everything goes wild in a standard farcical romp—Vera even goes after Marjorie with the power drill Dennis was using—which finally comes to an uproarious close as Pam slumps on the horn, giving the blast signal that brings Neil into the garage, on cue, turning on the lights and singing "Happy Birthday to you ———."

Vera to herself.   The last scene is the ironic anticlimax to a set of bizarre events. We are in the garden again despite the January weather. Vera sits huddled with a blanket up to her chin, very much in the same way we once saw the mother. However, there has been a complete role reversal; and Marjorie, in apparently renewed vigor, is now in charge of Dennis—and Vera. She bustles about, wishes Vera would be indoors to keep a better eye on her, and announces lunch for Dennis. Vera seems indifferent to those around her, apparently lost by now in her own world. She says almost nothing, looks up and away, half smiling to herself. When the others suggest she would be better off inside, on this her birthday, "tucked up at home," she softly answers "No." Dennis tries to counter the surprise of her reply by assuring everyone that she is "still disoriented."

The play thus ends with Dennis as unaware as before of Vera's real plight. It is obvious to the audience that in her near catatonic state, Vera would still prefer *not* to be in that house, under the eye of Marjorie; and is perfectly content, as it were, to be free of them in the cold January garden! This is a rather novel reading, one would have to admit, of the eternal dilemma of modern suburban life. With all the laughs and broad smiles, Ayckbourn has managed to have us thoughtfully and vitally concerned about some devastating agonies in the lives of his principals. Dennis and Vera and Pam and Neil are complete case studies of matrimonial disconnections. And the interesting question we should now consider has to do with technique: How did the theatrics work; how did Ayckbourn accomplish his "winter" comedy?

With some of the audience it was a delayed reaction. "One man laughed and laughed all through the play, as he told the author: it was only when he got to the pub that he suddenly felt very sad. That to Alan Ayckbourn, is the perfect audience reaction."[13] It would seem, then, that the Ayckbourn method is to surround us with the bare, often inane acts of human intercourse, laughable as they may be, up to the moment when they suddenly overwhelm us in their essential cruelty and waste. It is at these moments of realization in the play that we have the utmost sympathy with the innocent victims—the Veras and the Pams. When the laughter, as you might say, finally clears up, all we have left is the sight of Vera huddled against the winter cold—and everything else in life—completely cut off from Dennis's further "good" intentions.

The character of Dennis remains a frustrating dilemma to us—not wholly bad, not wholly good, or good enough when the demands are there, but still someone we find difficult to properly condemn. A number of times in the play his high optimism—his advice to Pam, for instance—has the right ring of truth to it. And yet we have the clear evidence, in the successive devastations that build up, that he is essentially a dangerous man, a motivator of events that will shatter the spirit. Michael Billington's review puts the finger fairly close to the central issue: " 'Presumably you've got feelings,' someone remarks to the hero of Alan Ayckbourn's *Just Between Ourselves*. 'Not if I can help it,' he retorts. And the gleeful, bovine irony that accompanies his reply is the most chilling moment in this singularly bleak comedy. For Ayckbourn is here writing, at his most mordant, about what Terrence Rattigan once called the real *vice Anglais*: fear of expressing emotion."[14]

Chapter Nine
Ten Times Table
and *Joking Apart*

Ten Times Table (1978)

Having tried nearly every setting possible around the home, Ayckbourn makes his first departure from the Home Counties and places *Ten Times Table* wholly in the Swan Hotel Ballroom for a series of committee meetings.[1] What we give up in not having the usual middle-class family tantrums is more than made up by the novelty of this underside look at the political passions that smolder in an otherwise quiet provincial town. The good fathers attempt to set up an annual folk festival in Pendon to stir up a little life—and a lot of needed business.

The chairman of the committee, Ray, has found an obscure reference to an obscure nonevent two hundred years ago in which the militia shot down a tax revolt. Thus, the festival theme, the Massacre of the Pendon Twelve, is born. But first and foremost, as the play's attraction, is the cleverness in setting four of the five scenes at committee meetings. The appropriateness is nearly as successful as the wise choice of Arthur Miller to set his universal drama, *Death of a Salesman,* on the salesman's life. Nearly all of us have been salesmen at one time—and, in the same inclusive sense, many of us know exactly what committee life turns out to be. Hours of interminable nonprogress, nit-picking on the minutes, sidetracking galore—and the inevitable clash of rival, quirky personalities. The possibilities for comic display are endless.

The fun begins at the committee's first meeting in November when Councilor Donald donates the services of his eighty-year-old mother, Audrey, to take the minutes. We can judge the alertness of the group when we consider that, after nods of gratitude, the issue is mildly raised about her deafness. It will work, they decide, if everyone turns in her direction since she reads lips. (This also allows the others to talk away from Audrey for private conferences—"off the record," one might say.) Amiability abounds as the meeting begins.

AUDREY. Could you ask them to speak down in this direction?

DONALD. We haven't started, mother.

HELEN. It's all right, my love, we haven't started.

AUDREY. You haven't started?

HELEN. No, we'll let you know when we start. We won't leave you out, don't worry. [*To the others*] Isn't she sweet?

The members of the committee include the chairman, Ray, who is the eager, enthusiastic one; Donald, particularly useful since he seems to serve on every other local committee, but here a continual obstacle with his attention to minute matters; Helen, Ray's wife, very outspoken and chipper; Eric, a bearded teacher, whose avowed Marxism will immediately set him off against the Tory lady, Helen; and Lawrence, a tight-lipped, burly alcoholic merchant. The meeting proceeds with periodic interruptions for a failing lighting system, and Helen's bristling complaints about the near-freezing room. The room has the opposite effect on Audrey who quickly struggles to remove her coat. "My God," Helen interjects, "the woman's an Eskimo." "Mother has exceptionally good circulation," Donald explains. When Ray begins to talk about the colorful past that they can commemorate, the Massacre of the Pendon Twelve, total silence reigns.

LAWRENCE. Of the what?

ERIC. Never heard of it.

DONALD. No. I can't say I have.

RAY. Well, it was a couple of hundred years ago. I came across it quite by accident myself.

DONALD. No, it's a new one on me. Mother might know.

HELEN. She was probably there.

DONALD. The Massacre of the Pendon Twelve, mother. Have you heard of it?

AUDREY. The Pendon Twelve? Was it recent?

DONALD. No, no. Some time ago.

AUDREY. No. Before my time.

The legendary past. Ray has found an account of these events in an obscure book entitled *Through Haunts of Coot and Hern*. The two heroes of the tax uprising were two local men, Jonathan Cockle and William Brunt, a strange contrasting pair. Cockle was a thin, clerical type; and Brunt, appropriate to the name, was a huge, hairy brute of a man who "would often for wagers toss his fellows high in the air." The introduction of these two farmers sets off a brisk exchange between Helen and Eric. Helen finds them both quite horrid; Eric defends them as hard working laborers, who couldn't help the way they looked—and who were probably "living at starvation level." Helen sees them as lazy and deserving their lot: "The trouble with them was they spent all the time making speeches. Getting drunk. Throwing people in the air. Serve them jolly well right."

The political line-up flares into the open. Eric, the admitted Marxist, takes this affront to the working man personally. He tears off at Helen, "What do you know, sitting there in your bloody fur coat, you stupid bourgeois bitch. . . ." More heated words—and Helen walks out. Other, lesser things happen before the first meeting ends. But we have the essential plot point of the play nicely (and colorfully) established. Two differing political views—the right and the left—will have it out through succeeding meetings. Ayckbourn's challenge, as some critics pointed out, will be the problem of making a satisfying mix of two divergent dramatic forms—the sitcom and the agitprop.[2]

Numerous elements of situation comedy are obviously evident throughout the play. One could say that Ayckbourn is such an old master of the technique that he can, with the wave of the pen, "resurrect" any number of required actions from previous plays. A little tailoring and they will fit the Swan Hotel Ballroom very well. There is no disgrace in this when done by a master as clever as Ayckbourn; however, a repeated complaint was that the results were adequate but far below the "inspired brilliance" of *The Norman Conquests*.[3] As far as the other part of the "mix"—the agitprop, the political views—there were few quarrels with the belief that for a first venture into such waters, Ayckbourn had done admirably well. It is possible, with a light vein added, to see these actions as state-of-England pronouncements. Of course, what matters the most is the way human inaccuracies are so well displayed.

The second meeting takes place the following month, in Decem-

ber. Eric suggests that they set up two divisions: one, "the proletarian faction represented by the Twelve," and the other, the military
faction (which causes the massacre). Helen, quick to argue on every
point—even the fact that Eric calls it a "rally" and she calls it a "pageant"—dislikes the plan. Visualizing the Kremlin in action, she sees
a plot to take over: "That's the way they gain their power. By dividing people up." Notwithstanding, the committee votes acceptance,
and we find Eric heading the proletarian faction and Helen, the
military.

The third meeting takes place in May. Helen reports that she is
having difficulty getting enough bodies to make a sizeable militia (at
least thirty) for the earl of Dorset to lead. Her contention is that Eric,
her rival, is luring them away. All his side needs, she argues, is
twelve, the Pendon Twelve:

HELEN.   I had planned originally on at least thirty soldiers. I mean,
         we need a minimum of that to make it look believable but
         every time I recruit someone, I find he's been lured over to
         the other side.

ERIC.   Mr. Chairman, I resent that.

RAY.   Yes, well, I know we've discussed this privately, love. I
         mean, you don't know that for certain, do you?

DONALD. Lured, Mr. Chairman? How exactly does Mrs. Dixon mean
         lured?

HELEN.   I'll tell you. By extremely underhand tactics. For instance,
         yesterday evening I had arranged a costume fitting for
         twelve very nice sixth form boys from the High School.
         And only two turned up. And they weren't interested. The
         rest had been lured away by promises of free beer and garish
         tee-shirts.

ERIC.   There is no proof of this, Mr. Chairman.

HELEN.   Oh yes, there is. Look at you, you're all wearing them.

To make things worse for Helen, Donald reports that the police have
reservations about the use of the earl of Dorset's horse. Riding a horse
through the market place "on a Saturday, with possibly many elderly
shoppers, an untrained horse ridden by perhaps an untrained rider
could constitute a hazard." Helen is ready to give up—"the only
thing I've got is a horse. . . . Well, that's it, isn't it. That's that."

Donald suggests a "stylised horse," a kind of hobby horse. Ray is inclined to agree, since "it's a pageant after all. We did agree at the
start we weren't going in for great realism."
    The voice of the people. When it comes time for Eric's re-
port, a number of doubts will arise about the realistic possibilities.
T-shirts have been made with John Cockle's likeness, which turns out
to be Eric himself, since he will play the part. Badges, car stickers,
and penants are on their way. "In short," Eric disclaims bravely,
"we're selling the name and image of John Cockle whenever and
wherever we can." And then, with little provocation, Eric launches
into a full panegyric: "It's to John Cockle we must look for our in-
spiration for this pageant. For it is John Cockle who represents the
ideals behind it. Cockle stood like a giant . . . a visionary if you like.
A man who saw that people were of this earth and that thus people
owned this earth. All people." To the astonishment of Helen and the
others, who might think they were in Red Square, Eric rises even
further in his appeal:

the natural birthright of every man, woman and child to sow the land and
to reap where they had sown without interference and without intimidation.
From anyone. . . . That words like landlord, tenant, ownership, land spec-
ulation would, in time, become as meaningless and empty as the capitalist
philosophy which lay behind them. And ultimately, the smallest—yes, I say
the smallest, most wretched of children would be able to dig his hand deep
into the raw dirt at his feet, clutch it in his fist and shout, "Yes. This too
belongs to me. . . ."

    Silence drowns the room, as Eric, followed by his supporters,
marches out. Helen is convinced of her worst fears. "The man's par-
anoid. He's cracked." Husband Ray meekly closes the meeting,
equally confused—"I don't know, we seem to be losing a lot of the
fun of this thing." At an emergency meeting called a few weeks later
by the militia faction, they decide to place their fortunes and their
success in the hands of Tim, Captain Barton, the no-nonsense dog
breeder. Not that he will restore "the fun of this thing," since he
hates Eric's guts on sight and is preparing a guerillalike frontal attack, but simply the fact that there is no one else.
    Captain Barton addresses the group in tight, crisp military tones:
he admits the strength of the enemy, considers their strategy, desig-
nates the room as the H.Q., and wonders where to conceal their
"dozen reliable men?" The plan, ultimately, is to conceal them in the

Reading Room, but not to frighten the older folks. "They can wear macs over their uniforms and conceal their hats till they get the signal. Then they strip off and into action." Others can be concealed (indicating the map) in the bus shelter, and "we could even stick a couple of chaps behind the War Memorial." The aim is to get Eric who will be on the rostrum.

The long prepared for Festival Day marks the riotous climax and end of the play. All that transpires is standard, quick-paced, ridiculous farcical action—and it must be judged that way. If successful, the action will catch the audience up in the mad whirl of events, and leave them fitfully laughing and content. There will be, therefore, in the theater house, little room for the careful cause and effect which proper comic analysis may require "the morning after." Good farce precludes such inquiries. And, along the lines then of the rules of farce, the scene does work. The two opposing forces—Marxist Eric on one side and Helen, Captain Tim, and the other "good people" on the other—clash as expected in open, physical combat. The meager forces of the militia faction are gathered in the Ball Room, without the expected recruits Tim spoke of. They rush out to fight with Eric who is completing his speech to his followers—the speech which means everything to him ("I'm only going to get a chance like this once in a lifetime"). And while we hear the offstage ruckus, Audrey, the deaf secretary, plays along on the piano, blithely indifferent to the mayhem.

The battle is joined. As expected, the events for Festival Day become a wild series of farcical errors. Everything possible seems to go wrong. The arrival of the horse—the hobby horse on its four wheels—is enough of a sad sight to discourage anyone. Although it sports a "proud tail and glassy staring eyes," the head has been somehow twisted around (Ray reports that he "bashed it getting out of the car") so that it seems to be trying to look over its shoulder. Nevertheless, they set it up for the planned diversion, and seat the muddled Lawrence on the horse:

> HELEN.   Now are you comfy now, Lawrence?
>
> LAWRENCE.   It won't throw me will it? [*He laughs.*]
>
> TIM.   Right. Open those crash doors, Dixon. We're launching the diversion. Stand by, everyone.
>
> RAY.   They appear to be shut.
>
> TIM.   Shut?

RAY.   They're padlocked.

TIM.   My God, it's them, the swine. Typical Marxist trick.
       Right. We're not beaten. We'll take him out the front
       doors. Wheel him out the front.

The quick wheeling to the other door is to no avail since these are
locked as well. Back they go to the crash doors, with Lawrence barely
holding on to the "proud steed." Tim, all defiant now, is prepared to
shoot the lock—which he does: At last, they shove Lawrence off
through the opened doors. By now the thoroughly giddy Lawrence,
overcome by drink, slides miserably off, doing "the slowest possible
sideways fall" and ending up underneath the horse. The failure of the
diversion is only the beginning of a series of comic mishaps.

The two forces race to meet each other. No one seems overly surprised that costumes that do not fit right are being patched on the
run by an energetic seamstress. The stage directions say it all: "Phillipa advances on Donald with a needle." Finally, the crazed Tim fires
away at Eric and wounds him in the leg; and Tim, in turn, is felled
by one of his own henchmen who waves a musket wildly around his
head but sees nothing with his glasses off. Even Helen, up to now
content to exhort the others on ("Let him have it. . . . Well done"),
is finally picked up and thrown by the man who plays the burly
Brunt. A touch of irony ends it all when.Audrey's research reveals
that the basis for the pageant was probably false. However, Ray's interest picks up again when Audrey says she *did* find out in her research that the Romans "met a very strong pocket of resistance round
here. From the Britons. Just on the edge of Pendon." More pageant
possibilities.

The "problem" in the play, strangely enough, lies in the excellence
of the four preceding scenes, the committee room business. They are
done so well that what happens at the end, the obligatory Festival
Day farce, is anticlimatic. How to satisfactorily resolve a comedy is
always a problem, as Irving Wardle points out: "As the comedy develops by polarizing the action between two fanatics, it is hard to see
how Ayckbourn could have avoided that last scene. But for all its
farcical energy and strokes of inspirational lunacy . . . it makes a flat
and noisy anti-climax to what has gone before: largely, I think, because Ayckbourn is not prepared to follow through the violent antag-
onisms he has aroused."[4]

The issue may well be *how* we would like to have the conflicts of character resolved in the play. A farcical explosion is one way to do it, but Wardle and others might have preferred a number of other, milder ways. The compliment, again, to the playwright, is that we may be so intrigued with the fun of committee procedures and their comic possibilities that we want more. The appropriateness to modern life is uniquely attractive, as Anthony Curtis illustrates: "Ayckbourn has managed to find in the divisiveness that afflicts every committee a perfect comic metaphor for contemporary England."[5] But then again, "comic metaphor," in Ayckbourn's experience, may require broad farce to make it succeed. Critical opinion, however, must always be comparative, and Benedict Nightingale reflects a growing view. "We have," he says, "come to expect too much of Ayckbourn and aren't happy unless he's somehow magicking water into wine? Perhaps. But if so, it's largely his fault, because it is he who has established himself as a trenchant social critic and even as a sort of theatrical heart-surgeon, capable of probing dark, subcutaneous secrets from his characters' mainly miserable lives."[6]

Joking Apart (1979)

Novelty abounds, one must admit, in the intriguing set Ayckbourn has devised for *Joking Apart*.[7] On one side a pergola placed above an interesting garden, and on the other, part of a tennis court complete with fencing and a workable gate. A brisk Guy Fawkes celebration is in progress with Richard lighting fireworks on the court with two small children, and the adults watching from above. All is very cozy and rural in a converted vicarage recently bought by Richard and Anthea, a thoroughly engaging couple, who, however, are unmarried, children notwithstanding. From their very first introduction, we somehow never feel the real urge to ask, Why? Cheeringly independent and such good fun, whatever they do seems easily justified. Their guests, however, will be an entirely different matter. We cannot ask enough questions about them.

The Reverend Hugh Emerson, late twenties, and his equally young wife, Louise, live in an adjoining property, once part of the entire estate. Newly arrived, only a few weeks, the Emersons bring their little boy, Christopher, to join the fun. Hugh is a stereotype clergyman, all apologetic and restrained; Louise is pale, intense, and seem-

ingly always in a state of half-fright. Everytime a firework goes off—
a banger—she screams and covers her ears. "She shouldn't really have
come," Hugh tells them, "She's absolutely terrified of bangers." She
will stay, though—and soon has another horror to deal with when it
becomes apparent what little Christopher is up to on the tennis court.
Anthea sounds the first alarm: "What on earth is your little boy
doing by the fireworks?" It seems that the little boy is relieving himself in the fireworks, and it brings down a chorus of recriminations.
"Naughty, naughty boy," Louise cries, and hurries him back to the
house.

Anthea has her own hands full trying to direct her children's enjoyment of the display—from a distance. "Giles, look at the colors,"
she calls, "Giles? . . . Honestly, the kid's half-witted. He's looking
in the wrong direction. Turn him round, Debbie, so he can see."
And later: "Watch the rocket, children. See? No, up, Giles. Up. It's
up there, you fool. Honestly."

Brian, a young man, employee of Richard's, has joined the party.
A bit morose and moody, he waits for his girl, Melody, equally upset, to join them outside. We learn that it is characteristic of Brian
to bring girls down for the weekend and then to have troubles. The
sparring way Melody will hand out food to the others and Brian
("You want some, lover boy?") makes the condition quickly apparent. "We adore you coming down here," Anthea chides him, "but
you always seem to bring down some girl you loathe the sight of and
then shout at her all weekend." This practice will be a running gag
that Ayckbourn will use in successive scenes as other girls will follow
Melody. There will be an additional complicating factor in that Brian
harbors a serious affection for Anthea.

Meanwhile, relations between the hosts, Richard and Anthea, and
Hugh are progressing much better. Since the properties used to be
one, the eventual division left the vicar with very little garden. Richard has a bold idea: why not knock down the rickety fence and give
their new neighbors a "look out at the garden [their garden] instead
of a fence." Before Hugh can say very much ("Well, it's—yes—I
mean . . ."), Anthea seconds the idea and Richard starts tearing it
apart and feeding it to the bonfire on the court. Amenities continue
between Anthea and Hugh while offstage we hear crash after splin-
tering crash in Richard's zealous labor. Occasionally, the edgy Hugh
interposes a cautious reminder, "I hope your husband knows what

he's doing. He'll stop when he gets to our house, will he?" Louise comes running to them, terrified that "there's someone round the back of the house breaking down our fence." Her logic in the following exchange is extremely interesting in what it tells us again of what Robert Frost meant in "Mending Wall"—"Something there is that doesn't love a wall":

ANTHEA. I think it's probably my fault—well our fault. We thought it'd be rather nice for you to use the whole garden, that's all.

LOUISE. But this is your garden.

ANTHEA. Well, yes but. . . .

LOUISE. Our garden was on the other side of the fence.

ANTHEA. Yes.

LOUISE. When there was a fence. Now we haven't got a fence so we haven't got a garden at all.

HUGH. Well, you've got this garden.

LOUISE. No, this is their garden. I'm talking about our garden. I don't want their garden. I want our garden.

Of course, Louise's argument is irrefutable. She is talking about property and basic privacy, views which tell us much about herself. "I don't feel secure without that fence. Anybody could walk into that garden. Anyone could look in through the windows." Pastoral responsibilities of Hugh's church—*their* church—seem to be a bit compromised with all this, as Hugh's sheepish apologies clearly indicate in the wake of Louise's tearful departure. "She'll be all right. She has these little tempers. But they're nothing. . . ." However, before Hugh can say his farewells, they are joined by Sven and Olive.

Sven Holmsenson is Richard's business partner and central to the basic plot, which involves essential differences between these two men; Richard is the charmer and great personality; Sven is ploddingly pedantic and intense about being always right. The progress of the play will reveal the widening gap between them, and, eventually, the comic frustration of Sven as he goes down to defeat. Before the scene ends, we have the chance of meeting Sven in action as he angrily insists that he is not an hour late, that he should not have missed the fireworks. Quite simply, Sven maintains, he was told 8:30 not 7:30.

After the introduction, Hugh still tries to escape, but Sven holds
him. A quick exchange on how long Hugh has known Richard and
Anthea ends on a curious note:

HUGH.   Delightful people.

SVEN.   Yes. Yes. Yes.

HUGH.   Well, that's certainly my impression.

SVEN.   May I say just one thing? As friends, be careful of them.

HUGH.   How do you mean?

SVEN.   No. I'll say nothing more. Be careful. Beware. That's all.
        Goodnight to you.

The art critic.   The mixture of the comic and the concerned
becomes apparent in the next scene, four years later. The use of farce
for psychological insight is well demonstrated here, indicating why
it may well be Ayckbourn's greatest gift as a modern playwright. For
example, we learn a great deal about Sven's complex character by
such "side excursions" as the opening comic business of the scene.
Another of Brian's girl friends, Mandy, is busily sketching, indifferent to all the social activity around her. Sven stalks about, making
what he believes are salient remarks about the art of sketching.
Mandy ignores him completely. Nevertheless, Sven quotes Picasso
and presses on. At the very end of the scene, he takes one more con-
clusive look at her painting. "Yes, yes. That is an improvement.
That is a great improvement. That is now a good picture. You see?
You can do it. Good. Clever girl." He leaves in smug satisfaction.
Mandy finishes her drawing, eyes it, scowls, and tears the picture
into pieces.

   This last ironic bit of business caps a number of salient revelations
in which we see how very jealous the others are of Richard and Anthea. Despite the fact that they are gathered again on a summer day
as their guests, the complaints begin to mount. Sven's wife, Olive,
expresses more real venom than humor in her constant reminders of
how thin Anthea is. And when it comes to the problems of raising
children, Louise and Olive conclude that their hosts are simply lucky
and even indifferent. "I mean," Olive says, "they take very little
trouble with them as far as I can see. They let them do very much
what they want." It seems unfair to Louise that her Christopher, now
eight, is so difficult to deal with. "I had to leave him to Hugh," she

tells Olive, "He's getting too strong for me now . . . when he punches you, it really hurts." We can draw our own conclusions when we learn elsewhere that Anthea's children, Debbie and Giles, plan to hide their toys "if Christopher Emerson is coming to lunch." Obviously, someone is doing something wrong.

The major contention is with Richard and the way he does business. Sven complains to Anthea that he makes "unilateral decisions which could quite easily have bankrupted the firm":

ANTHEA. Has he done that?

SVEN. Thank heavens, no. More through luck than good judgement, he has actually lost us very little. In fact to be strictly accurate, he has made us quite a nice little sum and . . . found us a new outlet. . . .

Nevertheless, Sven voices his complaint because Richard evidently was simply lucky and did not follow the usual business signs—"the known trading conditions . . . the present state of the world market. . . ." Most of all, he was leaving Sven out and his vanity could not stand this.

By the end of the act the rising dissatisfactions become a chorus of surprising jealousy. "She's certainly taken us over," Louise says of Anthea. "I mean, it started with just a helping hand but now they're running everything." There are now too many lunches and dinners hosted by Richard and Anthea. Sven has it all figured out: "They are nice people but they are invidious people. They have to take people over. And why? Because eventually they want to own people . . . and they do it in this very pleasant way."

The sour side of Ayckbourn's usual suburban frolics seems strange at first until we realize how effective the mixture can be. While we are witness to the many accusations against the golden couple, we also are spectators to the characteristic mishaps and mediocrity of the accusors. As Michael Billington points out, Ayckbourn "has created few richer or funnier characters than Sven . . . whose whole life is slowly eroded by his colleague's effortless flair."[8] There is enough characteristic bluster and petty silliness in Sven to escape us completely. And the fact that he increasingly blames his own misfortunes on others makes him an intriguing comic figure. The grand collapse will come eventually in a long-avoided tennis match with Richard. Up until the final moment, Sven has managed to trade convincingly on his reputation as a junior champion "three years running" in Finland. Anthea, however, has bothersome doubts ("I'll believe it when I see it"). While Sven has his usual rejoinder—"One day. One day. You wait. . . ."

The tennis match. Act 2, four years later, on a rainy, gray afternoon, features the long awaited tennis match. Another party is in progress at the house. A wild ridiculous doubles game has finally come to an end despite the light rain and strange tennis gear worn by some of the players. Sven arrives with Olive, both a bit heavier for the years. Richard goes off to change his clothers as Sven continues his disparagement of his business partner: "That man there, my excellent partner, runs the whole business in his sleep. He's never in the office . . . fails to read anything that's sent him . . . doesn't reply. And yet, yet, he thinks he knows more about the whole thing than we do who are there in the office working seven days a week. And the ironical thing . . . is that he does. Every damn decision he makes is invariably right." Olive finds it difficult to calm him; he feels completely unneeded—"reduced to nothing more than a piece of glorified office furniture."

A chance remark, however, made by one of the players, sets Sven off, and, yes, he will have a game with Richard: "Maybe in tennis I can still teach you something, eh?" So there, finally, on the worst of tennis days, the two adversaries square off. Of course, only Sven sees himself as a real "adversary," a determined avenger of his diminishing personal worth. Richard is as benign as ever, determined only to be a good host and to keep the cheer. The progress of the game, as already demonstrated in other matches, makes for interesting, challenging theater. We see a corner of the court and one player and hear the heated calls and movements across the way, offstage. The novelty for the audience is in catching the excitement of the on-lookers. In addition, we have the excitement of following a remarkable, often interrupted conversation between two of the on-lookers, a distraught Hugh and the buoyant Anthea. The fact that it begins with a breathless "Anthea, I think I have to say this now . . . ," gives us a small clue as to what is coming up.

The game proceeds with Sven as intense and struggling as ever. All are surprised that he is doing better than expected. Hugh continues to press the half-listening Anthea with the heat of some predicament—and finally, he blurts it out, "I am in love with you." Anthea is astonished. Over the last eight years he has come to admire her—

her unselfishness, her generosity. And it is not just a spiritual long-ing: "It's good old fully fledged carnal longing as well. For you and your body. For all of you." The game finally ends, remarkably, with a victory for the exhausted Sven. But then it all turns sour for Sven when someone reveals that Richard played him left-handed. "I thought he needed to win," Richard explains. Sven leaves disgusted: "At least you paid me the compliment of not hopping on one leg as well." The scene ends with Anthea sending Hugh home, promising not to mention this to Louise ("Oh no—never, never. I wouldn't—it would . . . no").

The last scene of the play, four more years later, ties things to-gether very nicely—"nicely" in the structural sense only, since we know the underlying gravity of the play and would expect no unreal-istic reversal in fortunes. Unlike the recent *Ten Times Table,* there is no need to resolve issues with a wild farcical ending. The proper end-ing for an Ayckbourn comedy is always a problem, and critics have differed on some over the years. I would suggest that this ending is one of the more successful. The dominant bittersweet nature of the play is discreetly kept. (No wild circus ending is needed.) Since time—the working of time—is an essential part of the plot, we see the principals fairly well as they must irretrievably remain. Somewhat as a soft coda might end the part of a symphony, we feel the propri-ety of the close.

The events are relatively simple; preparations for Debbie's eigh-teenth birthday party and another summer gathering of the principals to wish her well. Richard and Brian string lights and speakers on the tennis court. Sven and Olive arrive enroute to a holiday somewhere, Sven in obvious deteriorated condition, recently recovered from a heart attack. As the title tells us, all joking apart—with memories of *the* tennis match for one—we have our undeniable sympathy for him. He admits to Richard that by now, at forty two, he knows his limi-tations: "I am a man of only average ability. . . . I once made the mistake, Richard, of trying to compete with you." Richard, genial as ever, is nonplussed.

RICHARD. I don't quite see what I'm supposed to do. Sorry. I—

SVEN. Nothing, Richard. Nothing more than usual. Kindly con-tinue to support us all in the style to which we are accus-tomed, that's all.

RICHARD. [*Smiling*] I'll do my best.

A sufficient place to end *their* story. As for the Emersons, Hugh and Louise, the resolutions are both comic and grim. Keeping in mind Louise's earlier stage presence, what Irving Wardle called "a deadly study in the domestic tyranny of the weak," we have to smile to see her now, moving across the stage with glazed eyes, doped to the eyelids.[9] We assume that her problems have been many through the years. Nevertheless, the sight of her smiling incessantly at nothing is just the right broad comic note to weave through the entire closing scene. Partly to blame for her drugged condition are the facts about their precocious son, Christopher. As Anthea puts it, "He really is a weird youth when you meet him. You can almost hear this brain going around as he stares at you." The net result, she announces, is that he will not speak to his parents: "He's completely cut off from Louise and Hugh. He's quite gentle with them. He treats them like a couple of deaf-mute family retainers."

The final grace note—actually ironic—is provided by Sven's words of advice to young Debbie, in which he rambles on to her complete confusion:

Debbie, I just wanted to add a word, if I may. I wish you success, Debbie. I know you will have success because you come from a family which knows nothing but success. There are some lucky ones among us who we refer to as being born with a silver spoon in their mouths. You, Debbie, have been born with a whole canteen of cutlery. May I, on behalf of life's losers, those of us without a lousy plastic teaspoon to our name, ask you, please to accept humble greetings from one middle-aged mediocrity. . . . [*Olive starts crying*] Shut up, Olive . . . who has fought and lost. Remember if you will, Debbie, this saying: The tragedy of life is not that man loses but that he almost wins.

A complete silence follows except for Olive's sobs. Sven is completely spent. Totally exhausted, he seems drained of all further feeling. Debbie, characteristic of her age, is unsure what to make of all this. She does, however, manage after a few pleasantries about offered presents, to be quickly off and away from her parent's weird friends.

Robert Cushman's review, entitled "Not-so-funny Peculiar," makes some salient points. He is concerned about the comic effects: "The trouble is that most of the joking . . . is so far apart that it seems to be going on in the author's previous plays. The present one maintains his comic perceptions, but it is rather thin on actual comic moments." And in reference to the final picture we have of Louise, he says that "Her plight is not unlike that of the wife in *Just Between Ourselves* who declined in catatonia. The implication is that these are doubly shocking events because we have hitherto thought of them as comic characters."[10]

A generally common adverse opinion is that the work, for Ayckbourn, was only "a mild amusement." Milton Schulman expected more: "I could not get myself worked up about the futility of life at forty nor the social dilemma of unconvincing characters resenting failure."[11] *Country Life* called the work "elusive" and in need of a definite climax, "a turning point that is also a revelation."[12] Benedict Nightingale, however, took an opposite tack, attracted to the predicament of "painfully plausible people in a plausibly painful situation." Why, he asks, are there the many grudging reviews? It involves, Nightingale points out, two words, "preconception and prejudice": "For some, Ayckbourn is a bravura funnyman willfully denying paid-up audiences their quota of escape. For others, he is simply a commercial farceur with ideas above his station. . . . " His conclusion is that "the last scene is as good as anything Ayckbourn has written, justification in itself of his continuing attempt to darken his comedy and deepen our laughter." He goes so far as to say that the play may be Ayckbourn's best.[13]

Chapter Ten
Sisterly Feelings
and Taking Steps

Sisterly Feelings (1980)

Other Ayckbourn novelties aside—*The Norman Conquests,* for one—there is the strong view that with *Sisterly Feelings* there are still more structural challenges to be won for the playwright.[1] Clearly undaunted by past wizardry, Ayckbourn now presents what are essentially four different plays clearly encompassed into two evening productions with interchangeable scenes decided on the moment by the actors spinning a coin on stage.

In effect, the conception is simpler than it sounds in practice: two sisters, Dorcas and Abigail, are in love with one man, Simon. At the end of the final scene of act 1, they toss a coin to see who he will go with. They then play one of the two possible scenes—the "Abigail" or the "Dorcas" scene. At the end of the second scene of act 1 there will be another choice as to who goes with who. Thus, four different plays can be seen by the avid theatergoer, although two evenings will generally suffice to have it all. All versions end with the same brief scene which satisfies the central issue of chance in life. But the fun in the entire business is to play out *what might have been,* which is as much the tantalizing unknown as the offstages which comprise *The Norman Conquests.* As Jeremy Treglown points out, both Ayckbourn plays, along the model of "Stoppard's *Rosencrantz and Guildernstern are Dead,* are demonstrations of the idea that every exit is an entrance somewhere else."[2]

The play opens with a funeral and closes with a wedding. The single set shows us the slight rise of Pendon Common—also the setting for *Ten Times Table.* We see a steep grassy bank with planked steps cut in, which gives access to the view over the Common. It is late February, in the afternoon of a cold damp day. The family have just returned from a funeral, and Ralph Matthews, the bereaved, wants to show the others where he and Amy, the deceased, used to climb up to the bench to see the view. The entire family is present. Ralph's three children include Abigail (in a dull marriage with Patrick, a business tycoon), Dorcas, a BBC broadcaster (attached to Stafford, a shaggy poet), and Melvyn (with fiancée Brenda). Elders include Len Coker, Ralph's brother-in-law, a pompous detective inspector; and Rita, arthritic ("persecuted by fate," she says). The centerpiece for the plot is handsome Simon Grimshaw, Brenda's brother, divorced, available—essentially the stranger with a very "unEnglish tan."

Pendon Common has sentimental attachments for Ralph in his twenty-eight years of marriage; here, he proposed, here were the family picnics. He leads them up the hill, which presents us with a rather comic scramble of reluctant proportions. Aunt Rita needs assistance with her bad knee; young Stafford has to be urged up by Ralph who warns him that his smoking will give him soot—"he'll need to be swept." Why doesn't Stafford smile more often, Ralph asks Dorcas?

RALPH.   What is it? His stomach?
DORCAS.   No, his principles.
RALPH.   Oh, God help him. No cure for those.

Heroic Simon nearly bounds up the hill, to the mutual admiration of Dorcas and Abigail, who have already confessed to each other the blind ends of their own attachments. Rita, in the meanwhile, has fallen down a hole, and Simon goes to the rescue. The retreat from the hill, however, will have new complications.

Abigail's husband, Patrick, who has been loudly against the venture ("it's a bloody swamp") from the start, has warned them he must leave—and now angrily drives off. A problem is presented. How will the others get back, with only one car, Len's car? Some will have to walk. Both sisters are attracted to the idea of walking along with Simon. And now a nice comic bit follows in which they both keep saying "you'll go" to the other. Dorcas and Abigail stand adamant with Simon between them. Finally, Simon says, "Why don't *I* go in the car." He laughs, but they are not amused. Utlimately, they follow his advice and toss a coin. In this rather simple way, Ayckbourn manages to get his stage tricks going, to make the clever division into alternate scenes which characterizes the entire production.

In summary, the following are the possibilities: if Abigail wins the toss, we next play "Abigail's Picnic"; if Dorcas wins, we play Dorcas's "Picnic." Both take place the following June, and we assume in the interval that the romance with Simon has flourished with the one or the other. At the end of both picnics, there will be a rain shower which will allow the sisters to decide again if they want to continue with Simon or to return to the original arrangement—to Patrick (for Abigail), or the boy friend, Stafford (for Dorcas). The third scene, then, will either be "A Day at the Races" with Simon and Dorcas, or "A Night under Canvas" with Simon and Abigail. The fourth scene, the same as the prologue, remains unchanged. With Ayckbourn's usual virtuoso handling, all the scenes will neatly dovetail into their changing combinations, and the results will add up to a fascinating inquiry into the way chance orders our lives. It will come as no surprise that the last scene, "Footnote," will reveal the two sisters completely back where they started.

Abigail's picnic. In Abigail's "Picnic" it is a bright Sunday afternoon in June on Pendon Common. The day is a particular treat for Ralph as a way to keep the family together. By degrees they all arrive, notably Dorcas with the reluctant Stafford, whom she urges to socialize and not continually "walk away." Abigail and Simon have cycled over together and are an apparent close twosome. While Simon is off to fly kites, the sisters compare notes. Abigail is unsure about leaving Patrick, who probably knows the situation. Dorcas seems resigned to Stafford. The entire kite business at the top of the hill makes for entertaining theater. Simon and the others grapple excitingly with offstage kites, and in time this action will be the counterpoint to an earnest conversation about to begin. Simon shows Abigail how to handle the kite and she energetically works at the task while Simon, a little distance away, talks to Dorcas. The close nature of their long "huddle" begins to worry Abigail, and so we have the amusing picture of Abigail trying to coax her reluctant kite closer to the couple.

Our kite flyer has good reasons for wanting to get closer since she knows her sister too well. Dorcas is wasting little time in her conversation with the still desirable Simon. Starting with concerns about Abigail's welfare, she very cleverly maneuvers the conversation into a petulant examination of her own. She is a realist, she says, and not beautiful, which quickly brings a disclaimer from the entranced Simon. At last, Abigail has had enough—the wind tugs in the wrong direction—so she releases the kite entirely and throws herself unceremoniously between them.

However, the abrupt arrival of Patrick brings a new and more direct obstacle for Abigail. A full confrontation begins between Patrick ("how do we intend to sort this out?") and the highly nervous Simon. Essentially on a polite but direct level, the words fly around the bewildered Abigail as they keep referring to her in the third person. If they do decide to go off together, Patrick promises them a viscious divorce action; and "by the time I've finished with you," he heatedly concludes, "you'll probably have to sell both your bicycles." Abigail, visibly shaken, asks Simon what they should do. "To be perfectly honest," he replies, "I don't really know. At the present moment, I have a strong urge to go over there, wrap both his legs round his neck and stick his suede shoes in his mouth. But I suppose that would only be termed a temporary solution."

The picnic itself, with the passing of plates and sandwiches, and with the antagonism between Simon and Patrick, becomes the comic centerpiece of the scene. (By now in the Ayckbourn canon, meals of any kind are a standard comic device.) There are only so many plates, Dorcas finds as she hands them around, and Uncle Len does not have one. Simon, apparently, is the extra man. Patrick is quick to say, "Better hand in your plate, old son." In fact, he goes even one step further, and tears about a quarter off of *his* plate and hands it to Simon, who glares and clenches his fist. Again, trying to be careful with the sandwiches since Stafford, a vegetarian, will only take one with nuts alone, Dorcas passes them around. This still does not work out, since she runs out before she gets to Len and Rita. By this time, Abigail warns Dorcas that she is ruining her picnic. "Look," Len says, "I don't want to spoil anything, but I've got nothing at all." Of course, he never had a plate. Abigail, angry, empties Dorcas's plate and gives it to Len. Brenda complains that "it's a funny sandwich," a gritty one. In good, fast farce tempo, further "corrections" fly about, until, finally, Pat's gruff voice calls a halt to the merry-go-round: "Alright, own up. Who's eating Stafford's nuts? Come on."

The rain shower finally puts an end to the picnic and everyone scrambles for shelter. Now, again, there is a choice for the sisters as to who they will leave with. Some immediate factors might sway the heart since, on one side, there is Simon waiting in the rain with the two bicycles; and, on the other, there is Pat, neat and dry, offering his umbrella—"I say, can I give you a lift anywhere?" It is up to Abigail to decide, which she must do. And, then, accordingly, the third scene will be played, featuring either Abigail or Dorcas. Before we talk about these third scenes, a reminder about the alternate second scene, "Dorcas's Picnic." In effect, this will be a very close parallel to the other picnic, except now Simon is with Dorcas: and in the kite-flying business he will be distracted by Abigail and will begin to lean in *her* direction. The family wiles will prevail again in the exploration of *her* psyche, in such tempting lines as "I just know that given the chance there's so much I could give. . . . " She wants to give herself totally to a new life; and when the eye-popping Simon asks her to define what is her "all," she says everything, indicating her body—"all this, to put it absolutely crudely." This time Simon quarrels with Stafford, and when the rain shower arrives, the sisters will choose again.

Both third scene versions favor the original couplings—Dorcas with Stafford and Abigail with Patrick. It becomes obvious by now that Ayckbourn's intent with these plays is to show only the temporary distractions brought on by the attractive stranger, Simon. The point is philosophically made that even when left to chance the cross directions in our life will ultimately revert to rather normal channels. The diversions, nonetheless, in Ayckbourn's handling, become the ready sources of farce and comedy. This is proof again that "we are such stuff as dreams are made on." This, of course, is Ayckbourn's real country, the antic exploration of the inanities of life—the dreams, in a sense, gone wild and exuberant.

A day at the races. A few months further on, in September, we take up again the adventures of the two sisters. One variation of the scenes will be "A Day at the Races," featuring Dorcas in a full-blown farcical romp on the foot race staged at Pendon Common. All the elements are here for the practiced hand of Ayckbourn to have the most fun. Red and blue marker flags dot the hillside. Uncle Len, Detective Inspector Coker, to be exact, is in uniform, so to speak, with trench coat and arm band, cap, boots, stop watch, and whistle round his neck. Undoubtedly, the official for the event. Following close behind are Dorcas, Melvyn, and Brenda, dressed somewhat the same. They will be stewards. Len gives a graphic account of all their awesome responsibilities. He details how the runners will move at this, the last checkpoint before the finish—how they must go to the left of the red flag and to the right of the blue flag. The entire route, as Len goes over it, is a comic recital in itself, with the names of roads, junctions, and local (and amusing) place names.

The indefatigable Simon arrives in track suit, ready to compete. Dorcas is put out with him, because even though they sleep together, she has not seen much of him. His excuse is that he is preparing for the race. He thought it was his muscles and general fitness that attracted her. She says that is not all. Aren't he-men magazines popular with women, Simon asks? Dorcas corrects him:

DORCAS. Not for us—for other men!

SIMON. So. I'm wasting my time with all of this, am I?

DORCAS. How do you mean?

SIMON. Well, according to you, all I can hope to do rushing about like this is excite the other runners.

The subject of Stafford is an even greater source of contention between them. Simon openly insults him by calling him a "little maggot" and a squirt. A very different Stafford suddenly appears, wearing an impressive sporting cap and coat. He tells Dorcas that he is with the press, a new job, and covering the event. She only half believes him as he haphazardly seems to be jotting things down in a notebook.

Stafford, the would-be poet, has many of the qualities of Norman in *The Norman Conquests*. Ostensibly lazy and unreliable, there is still something attractive about him. He urges Dorcas to return to him; and despite her denial we sense a basic community of spirits. The key is in the fact that they easily laugh together—even in disagreement. Stafford relates how he faked references, using her father and even Simon to get the job. And this sets them off.

Len, ever worried, warns Dorcas away from the press. Something is going wrong with the race—no runners following the first two. He runs along side one of them, asking where everyone is. In an undertone the always politically sensitive inspector tells Dorcas what he suspects.

LEN. It would appear that we have lost the rest of the field.

DORCAS. Lost it?

LEN. Please. . . . Don't raise your voice. Our friend from the Press there will have it in the headlines two foot high. And

he'd love it, the bastard, he'd love it. It appears that van-
dals have removed one of our flags.

DORCAS. Oh no.

LEN. Causing the majority of the competitors to go straight on
up the B481, failing to turn off at the footbridge over Pendon Trickle. Thus, they have joined the A4155 with the
result they are, to the best of my knowledge, halfway to
Reading.

The scene ends with the race somehow coming to a conclusion,
with the exhausted Simon in a bedraggled "fall" to the finish line,
barely ahead of the eminent local rival. Looking on are Stafford and
Dorcas, very much a couple again, despite her misgivings about
nurse-maiding him once more. Nevertheless, they leave together,
laughing over the confessed fact that Stafford had faked the press job,
borrowed clothes and all.

The other third scene, "A Night under Canvas," features Abigail,
and again is set in September on Pendon Common. Abigail arrives
first, and is soon in earnest conversation with Patrick, who wants her
to return. Ultimately, Patrick says that he will wait till it is over
with Simon and then take her back. Simon arrives with full camping
gear as Patrick leaves. Abigail pleads for a complete "natural experience" in their camping out and protests against all the gear Simon is
setting up—even the tent. She takes the sleeping bag outside where
she can see the stars. Simon warns her about dew in the morning,
but to no avail; Abigail wants a memorable night ("let's go mad) and
says that she will take off all her clothes and dance for him. They
disrobe, but Simon, characteristically, is a bit wary.

A raid in the night. Ever watchful, Len, the police inspector,
suddenly appears with flashlights, a megaphone ("this is the police"),
and patrolman Murphy. Her clothes out of reach, Abigail runs for
the tent, as she is; Simon dashes up the hill. "No point in trying to
escape," Len says through the speaker. "The policeman now pursuing
you is a championship runner." Things happen quickly now to end
the scene. Patrick reappears and pretends to Len that they are simply
camping out. Alone now in the night, Abigail lures Pat into the tent
with a seductive bare arm.

The final scene, a month later, in November, is the same for all
versions. The wedding between Melvyn and Brenda has just been
concluded, and the family stops again at Pendon Common. Again,

the father, Ralph, urges them to the view, and again they all try, including Aunt Rita and her bad knee. The usual comic business follows. Abigail and Dorcas admit to each other that Simon was wrong for them, and that they made the right decisions. Dorcas, not entirely convinced, nevertheless gives the theme: "Yes, I expect we did. Anyhow, the important thing is for us to *feel* we've made decisions, isn't it. Otherwise, everything would just be so pointless." The play ends with one more choice. Who will travel home with the bride's mother and her big hat? "Tell you what," Dorcas says smiling, "I'll toss you for it."

Critical opinion on the play varies. It *is* Ayckbourn's most devious comedy, as the genealogy and map in the program attest to. And once the word gets around about the options in the scenes, there is an undeniable novel excitement as we wait for the actors to make their choices. It is a kind of theatrical dynamism which can be more than an attractive curiosity—a kind of instant theater. However, there are problems in the compulsion (which is good box office) to see two versions. I shared the experience of Mel Gussow when he pointed out that "two is one more than the average theatergoer need encounter. The first made me look forward to the second; the second made me realize that one had really been enough."[3] Since a number of actors must be so closely matched to their counterparts in the parallel scenes, there is the undeniable feelings that we have been here before. Probably the best way to enjoy the two evenings is to simply take each action as independent sketches, all superbly played by an excellent cast.

Robert Cushman would have preferred at least "one-head-on collision" for the two heroines, "rather than confining them to polite fencing with undertones; but overall this 'related comedy' [as it is subtitled] is excellent value," he concludes.[4] A deliberate lessening of the sisters' full characterizations may have been a price Ayckbourn had to pay to accommodate the structural gimmicks, as John Barber illustrates: "The intention . . . is to show how much people's lives depend on chance encounters and snap decisions. Excellent: but the idea is not pursued, and the sisters cannot engage the mind because they are seen *only* as creatures of impulse. The character drawing has to be shallow or the four-way permutation will not work."[5]

Most of the critics, however, were still willing to settle for the clever comic displays and not to ask too many carping questions about the further development possibilities of Ayckbourn's basic

premises, novel as they are. Jeremy Treglown echoed such practical
views: "The play for all its conservatism and light-weightness and
over-ingenuity, keeps the balance characteristic of Ayckbourn at his
best between comic optimism about the outcomes and a more cynical
gloom."[6]

And as for the concluding theme, in the last scene, where the sisters end up as before, what would Ayckbourn have us make of that?
"Is it a view to a life or a view to a death?" John Peter asks. "A bit
of both, actually. Dorcas and Abigail have their affairs but in the end
everyone ends up paired as before. It is almost as if Ayckbourn were
quizzically saying that neither chance nor choice can change a thing;
the family remains each time as we first saw it, in full possession of
its victims, its obsessions, and its insecurities."[7]

Taking Steps (1980)

It is quite appropriate that Ayckbourn's twenty-third play, an uproarious full-flying farce, be dedicated to England's grand master of
the form, Ben Travers, then a sprightly ninety-three and in attend-
ance ("The boy shows promise") on opening night.[8] To many critics
Taking Steps took the right step for Ayckbourn, back to basic farce
which some thought he had begun to desert in recent plays.[9] Ayckbourn summarized the plot himself, saying it was about "an attic, a
bedroom, a lounge, a wife in a quandry and a fiancée in a cupboard,
a devious builder, a nervous solicitor, a ponderous personnel officer
and a drunken bucket manufacturer all embroiled in a tale of love,
confusion and freedom."[10] This represents enough elements for a
number of farces, with the appropriate swinging doors, misunderstandings, general chaos, and mayhem dear to Travers's heart. Added
to these, however, is a novel element—most unlikely fifty years
ago—of a stage device that neatly telescopes three floors in an old
Victorian manor down to a flat one level. An ingenious set has the
six characters continually going up and down imaginary steps while
scenes are often simultaneously played on different floors. The net result is a forcing of the imagination—not a usual farce requisite—to
re-create a complete multileveled structure.

The play concerns Roland, a thrice-married businessman; the new
wife, Elizabeth, a dancer; and all the attendant problems in trying to
purchase the old house they rent while at the same time hanging on

to a fragile marriage. Movement, literally, is everything in a farce, and therefore the ubiquitous steps carry the principals up, down, across the living room, upstairs to the master bedroom, and to the servant's room in the attic. The play opens in the master bedroom with Elizabeth trying to write a letter of farewell to Roland while brother Mark commiserates. Amusements start early with Mark's fumbling attempts to read the note—considering Elizabeth's terrible handwriting. Mark reads, "I only wish I could have had the *cabbage*" when it should have been *"courage"!*

Elizabeth complains that she is being stifled by her husband's over attention; as a dancer she needs freedom to expand. This will be a running joke throughout the entire play, that is, her special needs as a dancer. The humor will be there even in the way she keeps saying I *am* a dancer. She defends herself, for example, on the issue of her bad handwriting: "I am a dancer not a writer." The issue is raised later when Roland complains that her bath perfumes are a bit much: "her muscle linaments . . . she was always covered in the stuff at bedtime. It was like sleeping next to a racehorse some nights."

Mark has his own complications with his girl friend Kitty. The history is appropriately bizarre: it seems that she abandoned him on their wedding day, ran off with a Cypriot waiter from the Boar Head (Mark still carries her honeymoon suitcase in the trunk of his car), and later was mistakenly accused of soliciting and escorted by the police out of town. Both parents will not speak to her, but, nevertheless, she is expected back. With such an introduction, we can hardly wait—along with lovesick Mark—to meet her. Elizabeth suggests that Kitty can sleep upstairs in the attic.

Enter now at the ground level Tristram, the young and very innocent solicitor, sent by his law firm as a substitute to help Roland with the purchase of the house. It can be seen now that we are rapidly assembling in appropriate farcical order enough diverse—"lost" might be the more accurate term—characters who will soon begin their varied misadventures in the house. Tristram's character will be tailor-made to the task. His trademark will be his fumbling with the language; ; "good morning" in the right order will be a challenge. The performance of Michael Maloney in the part was, according to Irving Wardle, a highpoint of the production—"solemn in suit and spectacles, spreading stupified bewilderment among everyone who tries to follow his beautifully-timed scrambled English."[11]

Enter Roland. Tristram's initial problem is to try to follow the chain of rambling thought of the newly met Roland:

ROLAND.   Well, what do you think of this place? What you've seen of it in the dark?

TRISTRAM.   Well. . . .

ROLAND.   Probably think I'm a lunatic buying it, don't you?

TRISTRAM.   No. No. . . .

ROLAND.   Yes, you do. Yes, you do. Don't blame you. [*More confidentially*] Listen. Business for just a second. Right?

TRISTRAM.   [*Alert immediately*] Yes, yes.

ROLAND.   This Bainbridge man'll be here in a minute. [*Consulting his watch*] I asked him to look in about . . . er. . . .

TRISTRAM.   This is the vendor?

ROLAND.   The man who's selling it. He'll be here in a second so let me fill you in. First of all, I think I've definitely decided I'm going through with the purchase of this place. We'll probably give him a bit of a dance first but I think I've made up my mind.

TRISTRAM.   I see, I see.

ROLAND.   The point is, you're absolutely right, of course. The place is totally beyond the pale. But you see, Mr. Watson, over and above a lot of things I'm a great believer in family. That make any sense to you?

TRISTRAM.   Oh yes. Your family are here, are they? From here?

ROLAND.   No, they're not.

TRISTRAM.   Ah.

ROLAND.   It's my wife's family. They're the local people.

TRISTRAM.   Oh I see. You didn't want to live where you were brought up.

ROLAND.   I was brought up in Singapore.

TRISTRAM.   Oh I see.

ROLAND.   Which is a hell of a long way to commute on a Monday morning. [*He laughs*]

TRISTRAM.   [*Laughing too*] Yes, yes.

ROLAND.   No, the point is, not wishing to bash around in the bushes, Mr. Watson. I've made a great deal of money. A great deal of money.

TRISTRAM.　Yes, yes.

ROLAND.　If you want to put it in those terms, I'm a successful man.

TRISTRAM.　Yes.

ROLAND.　No, to hell with it. Why not say? I'm a very successful man.

TRISTRAM.　Right.

ROLAND.　And very successful men, let's be truthful about this, very successful men should live in very big houses. Am I right? [*Tristram looks blank*] Or am I not right?

TRISTRAM.　[*Scarcely following the logic*] Oh yes.

ROLAND.　Otherwise, there seems to me to be no point in being very successful, does there?

The three-floors-in-one-set possibilities are fully introduced in the following scene: Roland and Tristram meet each other on the ground level; Elizabeth and Mark converse on the second floor with occasional ventures into the attic rooms. Although these playing areas must overlap, the definitions of the three rooms are kept by separate furniture and lighting. (The method is somewhat similar to the double set of *How the Other Half Loves*.) Whenever movement is needed from one floor to another, the actors mime the movement in treadmill fashion on the "flattened steps." Molding all of these strange mixtures into one hilarious entertainment is the characteristic challenge of the farce form. And there is never any doubt that Ayckbourn glories in the process; the requisite fast paced, never-look-backward romp is a structural as well as directorial achievement.

All the elements which will *mis*connect must first be carefully, rationally worked out on each side. For example, Roland tells Tristram about the history of the house; the place was once a brothel and rumor has it that one of the girls, Scarlet Lucy, was killed by one of the clients and is now the resident ghost. If she gets in bed with you, you will be dead in the morning. While Roland is telling this story with great gusto, Elizabeth literally walks between them, groping her way through the attic. Tristram remarks that he believes he hears someone walking about upstairs in the supposedly empty house. "Could be our ghost," Roland gleefully replies, already fairly awash with his usual neat whiskey nightcaps. He is an expansive, bucolic sort, determined to do things in a big way, befitting his position as a bucket manufacturer. The part is a tour de force for Dinsdale Landen, described by Milton Schulman as having a "military moustache, irate bearing, toothy smile, and vacuous mind of the men who lost the Empire and consumes whiskey like a distillery on fire."[12]

A legal brain. Roland's business conversation with Tristram starts and stops abruptly whenever it suddenly becomes apparent that, as a solicitor, Tristram is hopelessly a novice. Whatever he says becomes a jumbled alphabet soup; and Roland, in the grossest understatement of the play, wonders aloud if Tristram has a sufficient "legal brain." Meanwhile, with bags packed, Elizabeth is trying to steal down the ubiquitous stairs and out the front door. A number of times she is forced to withdraw and back up as someone approaches. The owner of the house, Leslie, arrives and the three men go off to tour the place. Elizabeth finally manages to escape.

Mark returns to the house with Kitty and leaves her in the attic. Some very careful "side stepping" follows again with everyone barely missing each other on the stairs and along the hallways. Vintage farce! A singular characteristic of the boring Mark is that his listeners invariably fall asleep while he is talking. Kitty obliges according to form—and we soon find her alone and asleep in the attic. Roland becomes upset when he finds the note from Elizabeth saying that she is leaving him. Many whiskies later, he is being comforted by Tristram and Leslie, whose only concern in this crazy business is to get Roland to sign the sales agreement. They persuade Tristram to spend the night, and we are not overly surprised that he is given Roland's pajamas to wear—and even his bed to sleep in. (A mistaken identity scene is being smoothly put together for us.) Roland rejects his own bed because of Elizabeth's overpowering perfumes, and chooses to sleep in the attic room. Kitty is awake now, having played the stair game to escape the house and lost; she finds herself backed again into the attic. How she is trapped there is a familiar stroke of farcical planning. As Roland enters the room, Kitty retreats in the dark and hides in a cupboard. The roof leaks and Roland moves the bed to avoid the water, thus neatly wedging Kitty behind the door for the duration of the mad night to follow.

Elizabeth has had a change of heart and sneaks back into the house to make things up with Roland. She deftly crawls into bed, assuming Tristram to be her husband, and stoutly—the dancer in her—holds on as the terrified Tristram tries vainly to escape the apparently deadly clutches of the ghost, Scarlet Lucy. By early morning, all positions—Elizabeth and Tristram, and Roland and Kitty upstairs—appear to have been maintained. A desperate Tristram hopes he may still escape before the dawn and thwart the legend. He taps a code on the floor for help which hurriedly sends Mark into the room. Brother Mark is horrified to find his sleeping sister so compromised. Nevertheless, English propriety still reigns and the discreet Mark even helps Tristram extricate himself from Elizabeth's grip. He replaces himself with a pillow which her arms clamp on, crushing it. "She's very strong," Tristram remarks. "She's a dancer," Mark reminds us. By the time the tongue-tied Tristram gives his explanation for the mix-up, Mark is inclined to believe it since he doubts that the solicitous solicitor has the intelligence to have invented it.

The best comic scene of the play enfolds now with the heroic attempts of Mark and Tristram—allies now—to awaken Roland from his deep sleep which they fear was induced by an overdose of pills in his despair over Elizabeth's leaving. They try to walk him downstairs as he awakens fitfully: "Bloody odd time to go for a walk. Middle of the night." Round and round the lounge they drag him, and finally, as a last resort, they sing and clap ("For he's a jolly good fellow") in their attempts to rouse him. Roland, half stupefied, not really knowing where he is, believes that he is talking to his workers at the shop as they cheer him on. He launches out into a full-set speech, the traditional management to workers salute:

> Now, it's about this time every year that we, the management, like to come along and have a chat with you fellows on the shop floor. . . . Now I'm sure it's true that every single one of you chaps must at some time— probably just as you're completing your hundredth bucket of the day, must have stopped and wondered what it's all about. And it's a perfectly natural question to ask oneself. What's in all this bucket business for me? Well, I can answer that in one phrase. Like everything else in this world, there is in buckets what you personally choose to put in them. . . .

By this time, Elizabeth has joined the melee downstairs, and manages convincingly to half-believe the garbled explanations offered to her. The nature of farce demands nearly implausible effects done by improbable causes. We would be led on the wrong track by the author if we were served up a heady supply of simple rationality. Enough pace and genial confusion in the production masks any sober attempts by the audience to attempt to add everything up. All that really matters in a good farce is a clever succession of broad amusements. The mixture is there for us to easily accept the next development in the plot in which Tristram and Kitty come to confide in each other, giving some indication of something lasting—or, at the least, the prospect of the befuddled helping the befuddled. Finally, at the conclusion, Roland buys the house and Elizabeth leaves again.

Some critics complained of the oversupply of farcical devices that finally wrap up the play, one being Mark's misjudgment of Tristram and Kitty when he discovers them exhausted and innocently asleep on the bed. We have seen nearly the same situation already with Tristram and Elizabeth. Bringing a farce to an end is always a problem, and it may well be that much momentum is lost "in the closing stages, when Ayckbourn seems to run out of breath and ideas."[13]

Chapter Eleven
Season's Greetings
and *Way Upstream*

Season's Greetings (1980)

Most general amusement Christmas plays have the tree ablaze with
tinfoil and lights somewhere on the set—a sufficient reminder of
where we are. However, with Ayckbourn much more than the usual
is always expected; and in *Season's Greetings,* with an adulterous couple
rolling about among the presents under the tree, we know we are in
for a bit more than the standard Tiny Tim greeting.[1] The farcical season is on again, and a number of carefully contrived sequences will
provokingly, pleasantly pass the time between Christmas Eve and
Christmas Day—"like a party that gets off to a good start and then
plunges into a cantankerous emptiness . . . the Ayckbourn obsession
with casting a shadow on his humor."[2]

Nevertheless, the outward elements of the play stay familiarly close
to the day's activities most of us would recognize—talks with relatives, the preparation of the dinner, the trimming of the tree, and so
forth. Our attention is easily held by a collection of interesting characters—and here, as elsewhere in vintage Ayckbourn, we have characters who are often more fully rounded than the basic farce structure
demands. Therefore, the critical problem many raise about the more
recent Ayckbourn plays is, where, if any, is the dividing line between
conventional farce and light comedy? Can some elements of each of
the forms be casually jumbled together?

The Christmas gathering at the Bunker home—a large, spacious
late Victorian—includes Neville Bunker, an easygoing retail manager, with his garage handyman obsessions; Belinda, his wife, becoming tired of the Christmas routine; Phyllis, Neville's alcoholic sister,
working on the family dinner between swigs; Dr. Bernard Longstaff,
her husband, "a rather faded man"; Uncle Harvey, a retired security

man and all-wise reactionary; Rachel, Belinda's spinster sister; and Clive, her invited guest. There is here enough of an engaging collection of familiar types to insure interest and genial hilarity.

While Bernard begins to set up his annual puppet show for the children, a fact which brings universal moans from the adults, Harvey gives a running commentary on the television fare (unseen by the audience), even to the extent of endorsing healthy violence for the kiddies. These two will be natural adversaries. Harvey warns Clive to draw a wide berth from Bernard as a doctor; patients, he says, have been known to die in his waiting room. He also blames Bernard for Phyllis's condition, which was bad enough before but is worse now. We have our own chance in the ensuing actions to realize that there are enough traumatic dispositions to easily go around. No one in the house is immune from the general condition of chronic self-delusion. As Linda Talbot explains, "Alan Ayckbourn has the knack of collating the calamities of Christmas. The lines . . . may be banal, the clash of personalities predictable. But being humourously confronted with the familiar, the audience goes home happy."[3]

In due time, the play settles down to a pursuit of Clive by the three women, a situation overly familiar from the recent *Sisterly Feelings*. The most humorous will be with the generally tipsy Phyllis. This is a scene which could benefit by enlargement since the relationship is quite novel: Phyllis bewails her pedestrian existence with Bernard and yearns for the world of Clive, the novice writer—he has published one book.

> PHYLLIS.   . . . Now. I want you to teach me all about English literature.
>
> CLIVE.   What now?
>
> PHYLLIS.   Please. Now. It's now or never. I realise I'm so ignorant. I'm thirty-nine years old, I know you wouldn't think that, but I'm thirty-nine years old and I want to know all about English literature before it's too late.

Reluctant Rachel.   Clive has no sooner shaken Phyllis off when Rachel, "his date," confronts him in the late night wanderings around the house when most are asleep. (There are periodic checks by the others on who is up and who is down.) Rachel launches into a full address—or confession—on her sexual orientation and present condition! She wants it clearly understood by Clive that at her age of thirty-eight there has not been very much sex in her life and that he should be fully aware that their relationship may only be Platonic. "I've managed without the other extremely well. . . . More or less. And I haven't honestly missed it and—well, I feel about it a bit like smoking—it would be stupid to take it up at my age and possibly damage my health when I've done so well so far."

Clive finally calms a sobbing Rachel while Harvey calls down again from the landing. Clive at last is about to retire when he meets another wanderer, Belinda, on her way to check the door of the deep-freeze. Rather quickly, her pent-up emotions flare ("Oh God, I want you") into a high centograde of instant desire for the hapless Clive. In good, high comic fashion she drags him from room to room to find the right place for their seduction. Not the sitting room, she says, "not in front of the television." Not the dining room and not the kitchen: "I'm not making love in a bloody kitchen. I'm too old for that." All the while she keeps saying that she loves him, "Promise me you won't leave me." Finally, they settle for the foot of the Christmas tree. What follows is excellent, well-timed farcical mayhem: Belinda throws her arms back, ready for him, and hits a musical toy which sets off a racket of noise throughout the house. In their wild, frantic search to discover which wrapped toy to silence, they open up a number of packages. Belinda opens one package with an awful pullover and is momentarily sidetracked, "My God, who's this from?" True to form, other disruptions follow. Switches are tripped and the lights and taped music go on. By now everyone is lined up at the top of the stairs. And this seems to be the proper place for the act to end.

In the final act we have the actual puppet show presented, which is of doubtful effect within the play. The critics seemed divided on this point despite the easy opportunity for some excellent comic baiting on Harvey's part as he hurries Bernard with the production: "Time you've finished, your audience will have grown up and left home." Even greater doubt, however, is raised about the final climactic scene, in which the gun-happy Harvey mistakes Clive for a thief and shoots him. It must be admitted that, as farces go, the audience will probably not question the matter too far since cause and effect can be neatly jumbled (and overlooked) when the farcical pace is just right—as it certainly is here. The string is run out when Bernard pronounces Clive dead and then, almost immediately ("I can't even get that right"), he is proved wrong with Clive's revival. Only an arm or shoulder was hit. They get him to a hospital as the play ends on a calm, naturalistic note with the others back to their own, little worlds.

The issue of comic reality and farcical mayhem still remains to cloud the evaluation of the play. It is a bit disconcerting once we have become involved with full realistic characters to have them suddenly shift to mechanical stereotypes. But then, again, credibility must always take a back seat to what *works* theatrically in the theater house. Literary analysis is fine for the study, but hand-clapping endorsements keep the playhouses open. And there is no doubt that there is clever handling involved here. As one critic ably pointed out in describing the ending, "Thus Ayckbourn jerks the face of this play emphatically to its farcical, lighter side, burning off the momentary tension like a smart lad tricking his parents into fear with a demonstration of his chemistry set."[4]

It is interesting to note how *Season's Greetings* got its start. Ayckbourn had first played around with the possibilities of doing a thriller, a real whodunit, but quickly gave it up. He did salvage two things for the play he eventually *did* write. He set much of the action of *Season's Greetings* in a hallway, a part of the house he had yet to use. Other plays have the kitchen, the bedroom, the garage, and even a tennis court. Why not a hallway? The idea appealed to Ayckbourn. As he explains, a hallway meant that "I had half a dining room and half a sitting room to put out their cigarette, or whatever, and they disappeared off stage—those rooms are sort of shadows. A hall is an interesting room because people are always passing through it on their way to something else."[5] The second thing he kept was the Christmas setting, which he had used before in *Absurd Person Singular*.

However, unlike the uproarious *Absurd Person Singular*, this play is meant to be a love story, something Ayckbourn admits that he has been trying to write for a long time. Of course, as the plot indicates, this is "a love story that goes wrong." All three women (Phyllis, Rachel, and Belinda) yearn for Clive; but, Clive being Clive, not much can really happen. His farewell to Rachel earlier sums it up: "Sorry I made such a mess of things. The story of my life. Every time something of value comes along, I—."

Way Upstream (1982)

Picture, if you can, the man in charge—Alan Ayckbourn of course—sitting idly one day in his theater pondering what further challenges he can tempt his familiar "floor boards" into. By now he has tried almost everything; but, he is caught by the singular fact that, unlike most stages, his has a sturdy concrete floor. And from this simple notion comes the idea for the most original set Ayckbourn is to devise—an actual riverbed which he can flood to ten inches of water (20,000 gallons) and on which he can move a full-size boat (a twenty-four-foot cabin cruiser) realistically around. Nothing could suit Ayckbourn's idea of theater better than to take on such a project ("outrageous," one local critic called it) and to produce the illusion complete of a cabin cruiser meandering slowly down the river, through locks, and even gurgling under a bridge. The actual task, of course, was given to the young company set designer, Edward Lipscombe, who earned deserved praise for the result.

Way Upstream thus becomes an almost unbeatable attraction as Ayckbourn's twenty-sixth play.[6] No one seems over concerned if the boat actually steals the show since good theater unabashedly leans that way. The audience can be properly intrigued by a number of clever gimmicks, reminding us that there is more circus and show than we realize in good modern theater. (Consider the plot of David Storey's *The Contractor* of 1969, in which much of the interest is in the putting up and taking down of a party tent.) However, Ayckbourn's enchanting boat is only the first of a series of surprises, as Robin Thornber points out. Visually, it may be "a commercial for the Inland Waterways Association," but it is also, philosophically, "a plug for the soggy centrism of the Social Democratic Party."[7] For the first time in his career, Ayckbourn gives us a clear political statement. Not since the hijinks of *Ten Times Table* with its left and right adversaries do we have anything so explicit.

The play concerns the misadventures, in standard Ayckbourn fashion, of two couples on a seven-day journey down the River Orb, heading, appropriately enough, for Armageddon Bridge. By the time they arrive, the temper of the drama has changed from rueful comedy to hard realism bordering on fantasy with mutineers taking over the ship—and a belated hero somehow established. The couples are a strong contrast: the two men are partners in a novelty goods factory, with one, Keith, bossy and assertive; and the other, Alistair, meek and deferential. The women, likewise, match up: Keith's June is a nymphomaniac and Alistair's Emma is hesitantly mild and subdued— or, as Anthony Curtis aptly puts it, "a contrast between the predatory and the pure."[8]

The first half of the play has familiar Ayckbourn items, a kind of floating *Bedroom Farce,* with excellent opportunities to contrast the two couples trying to play mariners and barely succeeding. "Boats are a society in miniature," says Keith. "Everybody has a role, everybody has a function." As the company director on land, Keith sees nothing inconsistent in assuming the post of captain of the ship. The fact, however, that he has never sailed and has only read up on it seems unimportant. Alistair meekly concedes, as does Emma, though she wisely wears her lifejacket most of the time. June, however, is not satisfied and maintains the marital discord at a good farcical pitch throughout. Internal vexations meet outer ones with the daily visitations of the company secretary, Mrs. Hatfield, who brings news of the worker's strike ("trouble at t'mill"). Keith eventually goes off to handle the takeover manfully, leaving Alistair to quickly run the boat aground.

At this point the play (and the boat) veers sharply from "Pineroland and enters J. M. Barrie country."[9] They are forced to take aboard the sinister but strong Vince who frees them from the mud while coarsely taking over Keith's wife (ready and willing) and the boat! He even renames the boat and its crew. He is soon joined by his rich and decadent girl friend, Fleur, of a titled family. Together they get rid of Keith and transform the pleasure boat into a "pirate ship" and even a torture chamber.

A brutal fantasy. "Though the audience wants to go on laughing," according to Hermione Lee, "there is nothing good-humored about this part of the play. It's a simple, brutal fantasy about the ease with which fascists, or anarchists, or extremists, can take over and abuse the English middle-classes based to a large extent on the dislikeable assumption that women are turned on by macho violence."[10] The abuse, physical and otherwise, continues until the worm suddenly turns—the acquiescent Alistair draws the line when the mutineers attempt to make Emma walk the plank. Somehow, they overcome the enemy and the pirate flag is replaced with a Union Jack, the point being strongly made that the English by temperament will take ill manners and evil only up to a point and then rise manfully against it.

The role of Alistair, then, becomes the familiar one in the Ayckbourn canon of the antihero, the sometime bumbler, along the lines of Norman in the *Norman Conquests* and Leonard in *Time and Time Again,* who ultimately see things better than the rest of us. Even when not entirely convincing, such Ayckbourn major creations always have the best lines, although at times a bit limited. Here, with Alistair, we have what Desmond Pratt calls "one of his [Ayckbourn's] wonderful semi-speechless studies of the ineffectual hesitant flounderer."[11]

Nevertheless, there is a critical disagreement on how successful this transformation is in the resolution of the play. Gerald Clarke, writing in *Time* of the American premiere, sees the character of Alistair as the primary problem: "he is, despite appearances, the center around which everything turns: he is, the author seems to be saying, the country's true salvation—if he can be made angry enough. Unfortunately, his passivity defeats even his creator and his belated transformation from mouse to man at Armageddon Bridge seems more like a miracle than an authentic development of character."[12]

It may well be that the quick resurrection of Alistair into a hero needs no realistic defense if we have been already fairly well drawn along into the fantasy of the mutiny itself. Improbabilities have never been a bothersome Ayckbourn concern once the rhythm of his special kind of theatrics begins to hum along. There is no better indication of the way Ayckbourn works his stage than his daring conclusion to the action. As our victors, Alistair and Emma, finally emerge alone on the boat into the sunlight at Armageddon Bridge, they strip completely, and in full frontal nudity they simulate a dive into the water.

The local Yorkshire press made much of Ayckbourn's first use of nudity on stage ("a cheeky end"), but the London press took it in stride, as they well should. It was not intended to titilate the audience or save a sinking play, as is often the case today; the action fits the integrity of the play completely if we recall the Garden of Eden symbolism present throughout the play. From the start, the point has been well made that Alistair seeks an "ideal holiday" in sharp contrast to the public rowdiness of Keith and June. Their eventual success and escape is the reward of their essential innocence—and the nude dive into the water as they hold hands is paradise enow!

Far more debatable is the questionable last words Alistair has as they both size up what might be the political-philosophical basis of their terrible ordeal. Once saved, Emma says that they should not go back; they are all so unreasonable. Alistair replies, "Then we reasonable ones will have to go back and reason with them." This has a nice sound to it, but one wonders how it fits their present actions. So says Hermione Lee, pointing out that "hitting your enemy on the head and running for your life has earlier seemed to be the only effective form of securing a decent civilized society" and thus "this final moral has a hollow ring."[13]

A strong political view may be Ayckbourn's primary concern, but the general attitude of the audience seems to be to simply sit loosely in your chair, watch where you walk during the breaks, and enjoy the fascinating boat which still steals the show. Whatever it does, it commands the audience's attention. They greet every minute detail (the change of light as the boat passes beneath a bridge, the passage through the locks) with applause. For a seafaring nation Ayckbourn has an easy winner.

Chapter Twelve
Summations

The Well-made Farce

Ayckbourn would be the first one to admit that comedy is difficult enough to do without having to explain how it works. And the thought that some day his plays might be the subjects of academic dissection would certainly make him smile. All are understandable views from his standpoint since Ayckbourn is fundamentally an entertainer, a fortunate all-theater man who knows to the core what will work on the stage. He has the actor's feel—and the director's sure hand—in sensing what material will make us laugh. Nevertheless, everyone concerned with good theater will still persist in asking the necessary questions about Ayckbourn's art of comedy. Twenty-eight produced plays of varying quality, many now playing continually around the world, is a major achievement.

The first West End success, *Relatively Speaking,* is "thoroughly old-fashioned," a deliberately written, well-made play. "It is a piece of machinery," Ayckbourn admits, "that ticks away whether the actors are actually driving or not."[1] The form, of course, is the farce, an old and reliable formula for laughter that Ayckbourn makes completely his own in a number of notable plays. Traditionally, farce is a low kind of comedy in the way that melodrama is a low kind of tragedy. Both forms are usually deliberately thin on plot and character and heavy on improbable situations and gross incongruities.[2] The chief aim of farce is laughter at any cost—and everything must give way to it. When done properly, at the right commanding pace, the audience never has time to ask about cause and effect or why the hilarious events are as they are. The sound of laughter is the only raison d'être of the well-made farce.

Ayckbourn's distinctive contribution to the form is in his keen knowledge of the wide English middle class and their characteristic polite deferences and hesitancies. The famous British "unflappability" in the face of mounting incongruities makes the basic farce almost a national institution. In *Relatively Speaking* the young couple, Ginny and Greg, individually gain quick acceptance into the country home of the elders, Sheila and Philip, simply because it would be impolite to turn them away. The assumption is always that there was some antecedent action (or business) that the "host" missed and that it would be "good form" to pretend full knowledge. Of course, these initial evasions of *open* embarrassments will lead to the usual mounting series of *closed* embarrassments which make the evening's laughter. Ginny's pretense to being Philip's daughter is the kind of high wire act that holds the audience in laughter—and wonder. The cleverness of the script keeps everyone on edge wondering when and where the slip will come that will bring everything crashing down. It is also interesting to note that there must be some universal (more than English alone) human frailities and misadventures in the play that makes it such a wide, international favorite.

By the time (1977) Ayckbourn produced *Bedroom Farce,* ten years of productive stage experimentation with farce had elapsed—ten years in which the form had been used *in part*—and Ayckbourn was ready again to try it completely. The intervening years saw a number of farcical scenes in various plays. The dominant form by now, of course, was conventional comedy. There was never any doubt from the start that Ayckbourn intended to go beyond the usual one-dimensional characterizations of standard farce. The result would be engaging (as well as amusing) portraits in English suburbia—the overbearing, the failures, the up-and-coming, the neglected, the guiltily promiscuous, to name only a few. However, all-out farce remained a convenient form, at times, to hurry the comedies to a close.

Such is the case in the extremely successful *Absurd Person Singular.* Since each of the three acts—which portray three different Christmases—is somewhat independent from the others, there was no marked inconsistency in having the third act turn into a wild romp. Sidney leads the others in a mad party game in which he forces them to act as complete fools. However, the audience's easy amusement in the quick-stepping action is soberly tempered with the realization of what the ambitious Sidney has finally come to. These concerns, of course, are full character recognitions drawn from one act into another, reminding us that the play is still essentially an integrated comedy. Another excellent illustration of the "descent" into farce is in the conclusion to *Ten Times Table* in which the long planned Pendon Massacre commemorative festival turns out to be nearly a literal massacre of the principals.

Bedroom Farce, as the title indicates, is wholly within the form. By now, Ayckbourn has the experience and the mastery of technique to move everything along in a near balletlike mathematical precision. The device of three bedrooms across the stage allows the necessary shifts and interplay between the three resident couples and the roving visitors of the night, Trevor and Susannah. And the novelty of the "static" settings greatly increases the fun since we are to be artfully informed (as well as amused) in the new possibilities of bedrooms. Malcolm, for example, decides at two in the morning to put together a table kit in the bedroom since they have to stay up for Trevor anyway. It is the piling up of ridiculous situations—one more absurd than the other—that makes a complete farce into a complete, hilarious evening. We shift quickly from bedroom to bedroom and there is no end to it. While Jan and Nick are tumbling all over, trying to extricate themselves from the strange entrapment of Nick's bad back, the older couple, Ernest and Delia, are turning their bed into a smorgasbord.

The Art of Comedy

It seems that with Ayckbourn the dividing line between farce and comedy is a matter of the overall composition of the play and whatever strong intentions, if any, are essential to the play. Not surprisingly, plays with novel staging such as *Bedroom Farce* and *Taking Steps* (with its imaginative stairways) derive nearly everything from the playwright's clever handling of the new possibilities. The generation of laughter, quite naturally, takes precedence over any social commentary. These are the successful farces and need no other apology for their existence. The comedies, on the other hand, have other centers of development, such as the irrepressible Norman in *The Norman Conquests,* who is determined in his own zany way to bring happiness into the droll lives of the women he "conquers."

What makes the trilogy so successful are the many avenues into our present lives that Ayckbourn is able to explore. In a full Chekhovian manner we have our domestic misfortunes delightfully thrown back at us in the course of one mad weekend. Annie, the stay-at-home sister, has all the right answers for her would-be wrong behavior. Her frustrations are intensely real ("haven't been away from this place for nearly two years"); her solutions are comic marvels: "What the hell," she agrees with Norman, "let's do what we said and have a really *dirty* weekend. I mean absolutely *filthy*. . . . God, I'm putting this awfully badly."

When we add in the plight of the two other "sisters" (Ruth, *the* sister, and Sarah, the sister-in-law), we do have a kind of ribald Chekhov's *Three Sisters* (1900). In place of the sisters' mutual plea "let's get to Moscow," the uniform yearning here may well be "let's get to Norman." In some of Ayckbourn's cleverest writing, he somehow manages a full reversal of the bleak repute his wife, Ruth, and Sarah hold for him. Both women are excellent portraits of suburban dilemmas: the ambitious wife who suffers the indolent husband, and the self-martyred wife (Sarah) who suffers everything.

Joking Apart is another masterful exploration, in an insightful Chekhovian manner, into a complete milieu—the fairly comfortable life of Richard and Anthea and the many friends and neighbors they affect over a twelve-year period. Of course, to Sven, the by-passed business partner, and to Louise, the distraught neighbor, the influence is more an *infestation* that they are helpless to avoid. The "good works" of the couple—with their insistent jollity and disingenuous warm intentions—are like some benign afflictions which, in time, will do them in. Ayckbourn's cleverness is in his honest presentation of the couple as basically good on the one hand, and the equally full demonstration of their detractors' enmity, jealousy, and hysteria on the other hand. In the breach between these extreme positions lies comedy.

The fact that *Joking Apart* had the shortest run (four months) of all the major plays gives us some indication that Ayckbourn was evolving a new and more demanding comic style for himself. The general audience was, quite frankly, a bit confused in Ayckbourn's departure from straight forward comedy—this despite another *Plays and Players* award (shared) for Best Comedy of 1979. During these years, from 1975 to 1979, Ayckbourn had deliberately begun to deepen his plays, what he now refers to as his "winter" plays. Beginning with *Absent Friends* and continuing with *Just Between Ourselves* and *Joking Apart,* we have what Ayckbourn calls the "truth" of comedy as well as the 'fun."

Bittersweet Truths

The accomplishment of *Absent Friends*—to many, his finest play—
is the arrival to a degree of ability in comic writing that moves Ayckbourn closer to the master playwrights. It may succeed in adding
more firmly the term, "human," to the general phrase "human comedy," perhaps in the sense that Balzac used the phrase to indicate a
complete rendering of human existence. We are comic, both writers
are saying, because we are essentially human, and nothing less. Ayckbourn is able to bring out some terrifying truths about the human
condition in this comparatively simple play. The truths, however, are
bittersweet and can provoke laughter as well as tears. Although the
entire play centers on the bereaved Colin who needs no bereavements,
it is his effect on his friends in bringing out their true lives that is
the real accomplishment of the comedy. Ayckbourn admits that the
play was a "small progress . . . towards my unattainable goal: to
write a totally effortless, totally truthful, unforced comedy shaped
like a flawless diamond, in which one can see a million reflections,
both one's own and other people's."[3]

The above comment was directed as much to *Just Between Ourselves*
as to the earlier play. He was thoroughly aware how daring it would
be for a comic writer to end the play with the principal, Vera, in a
complete catatonic state. Not the usual happy ending his audience
and his critics expected. However, again, the intention of the play is
along Chekhovian lines—to reveal ourselves to ourselves. Ayckbourn
explains: "Dennis, the husband, is no calculating villain. Nor is he,
I contend, particularly unusual. Just a man pathologically incapable
of understanding beyond a certain level. His wife's cries for help go
unanswered not because he ignores them or fails to hear them, but
because he honestly hasn't the slightest idea what they're about."[4]

The reason why Ayckbourn the Serious and Ayckbourn the Comic
work so well together is because no matter how much "truth" he increasingly adds to his plays, the "fun" always goes on. In Ayckbourn's plays amusements are always present in even the smallest of
events, so that there is never an overreaching in plotting to encom-
pass the two extremes. Guido Almansi sees the process quite clearly:
"it is essential to pitch the action low, down to a base line of utmost
banality. The events must ultimately be non-events so as to astonish
us with the incomprehensible preoccupations of the characters. The

more trifling the occurrences which make the plot move forward, the
more hilarious is the shattering effect that these minimal disturbances
have upon the emotional lives of our heroes."[5] Therefore, there are a
number of disastrous (and comic) meals, big and small, which fre-
quent the action in the plays. When staged properly, these "confrontations at the table"—the arranging of seating, the passing of cups
and napkins, the handing around of sandwiches—become mountains
of hilarity and frustration.

Other trifling actions are concluded in slow, meandering ways, all
the while bringing out important traits of personality. The basic
power structure within a family can be amazingly well revealed by a
series of comic nonevents. Language as well as stage business can be
effective nonevents. Notice in the following exchange between the
desultory Brian and his young girl friend in *Joking Apart* how much
is revealed of their failing relationship:

> MO.   You wouldn't understand if I told you.
>
> BRIAN. Why not?
>
> MO.   You're too old.
>
> BRIAN. Too old?
>
> MO.   You're over thirty.
>
> BRIAN. What's that got to do with it?
>
> MO.   If you're over thirty, then you're too old. You've forgotten
>   what it's like.
>
> BRIAN. What what's like?
>
> MO.   To be under thirty.
>
> BRIAN. Oh, great.

Another example, in "Table Manners" of *The Norman Conquests:*
Norman is angry at his wife, Ruth, and resolved to tell her about the
planned weekend with Annie. However, Ruth, who has misplaced
her glasses again, doubts his every move in their animated conversation:

> NORMAN. Do you want to know what I'm doing here? I'll tell you,
>   shall I?
>
> RUTH.   If you want to.
>
> NORMAN. I will tell you. [*He rises*]
>
> RUTH.   Where are you going?

NORMAN. Nowhere. I'm just standing up.

RUTH. Well, sit down, I can't see you properly.

NORMAN. This has to be said standing up.

RUTH. What is it, the National Anthem?

As Almansi points out, "There are occasions when a sequence of trite words has more bite than a well-turned phrase or a brilliant metaphor. Ayckbourn knows how to operate dramatically on what seems to be utterly banal: which is certainly more difficult than the exploitation of the sublime."[6]

Character Studies

We are not surprised that a number of the major plays are essentially character studies of engaging personalities. Such is the case with Leonard in *Time and Time Again,* Norman in *The Norman Conquests,* Colin in *Absent Friends,* and Dennis in *Just Between Ourselves.* Each of these characters puts his indefinable stamp on his own ground, his unique portion of English suburbia. They are all marvelously complex. Leonard, the ex-teacher, is a determined independent who fails to see how very dependent he really is. When his girl, Joan, finally despairs of him at the end, it is an insightful recognition of the hopelessness of his passive condition. She can not follow his ways: "we don't all happen to be bloody poets, do we." Nevertheless, we have been charmed in the course of the play by his baggy-pants demeanor and infectious good humor. Possibly, as the critics said, another Hamlet of the byways.

Norman, on the other hand, is a man of action, a full romantic, determined to be the catalyst in the resurgent affairs of others. There is no doubt that Ayckbourn needs all three of the plays in the trilogy to bring out the many aspects and adventures (and misadventures) of our Don Quixote. In the sense that a good novel brings out all of life, we have the possibility here in a play of this size to learn a great deal about the world of Norman. In the same sense, although with less scope, in *Absent Friends* we have the chance to understand Colin and the world *he* affects. Somewhat as a missionary from another land, Colin returns to his friends after many years, bearing a new hope ("I've always fallen on my feet, you know") which startles everyone. In some of Ayckbourn's most challenging writing, he manages to give us considerations of the fact of death which are continuously funny—and never morbid.

And then there is the world of Dennis in *Just Between Ourselves*. He makes a fascinating centerpiece of passive geniality, somewhat like Leonard in his basic inaction (when the opposite is desperately called for), but actually a more complex figure. Unlike Leonard, Dennis really believes that he has properly found his center-stage position— between his wife and his mother—and never doubts his complete adequacy in all mature matters. (Part of the charm of Leonard is his eternal, essential boyishness.) In this sense, Dennis may be a more familiar figure in our lives, in that he is so certain of himself when he is often so very wrong. Considering what he does to Vera, he may be the most dangerous, as well. A number of times in the play, he will respond characteristically with quick confidence—and then give us the feeling that perhaps he missed something. These are fleeting moments (or indications) but they work well in suggesting a rather terrifying condition of what could be called mindless philanthropy.

Ayckbourn draws some of his best comic portraits with two contrasting types—"the male bumblers" and the "men in charge." The outsiders and the insiders. Peter, the accident-prone athlete in *Time and Time Again,* is a bumbler of the first order, even beyond the physical scrapes. As Leonard's contender for Joan, he seems amazingly unaware of what is going on—even in the midst of Leonard's wedding plans. Perhaps it is appropriate at the end, when Leonard has lost Joan, that they seem to have each other. It may well be that Tom, the veterinarian in *The Norman Conquests,* is the most satisfying comic figure Ayckbourn has created. Again, the size of the trilogy adds immeasurably to our full knowledge of the man. Long after the plays are memory, Tom's characteristic "Ah-sounds" linger on—these somber "pronouncements" which indicate that some vital bit of communication is trying to make its desperate way through his dim consciousness. Taken as a whole, it is a marvelous portrait of literal, small-minded man. The scenes with Annie, in which she tries to strike some romance between them, are some of the funniest. "It'll come to me," Tom says, as they try to make conversation. "Don't force it," Annie wearily counsels.

Unlike Tom, who is limited in resources, Trevor *(Bedroom Farce)* is constantly ready for self-analysis. In the modern parlance, he is always "couch-ready," with a full assortment of terms and psychic conditions to throw at anyone who will listen. We are not surprised, in the thin plot, that the presence of all these beds is such an irresistible attraction. Trevor, literally at full length rattling off his angst, becomes the expected after awhile. (He almost does as well as Goldilocks in sampling the three beds.) Nevertheless, in his mindless foolishness he qualifies as another "bumbler." Tristram's problem in *Taking Steps*, among other things, is language. And here Ayckbourn is able to work up some effective scenes of almost complete incomprehensiveness. Roland meets Tristram, the substitute solicitor, for the first time. Tristram explains: "I've got the contractual finalisations—er—the finalised contracturals—rather contracts—ready. So there should be no obvious . . . er . . . er . . . er . . . oh . . . er . . . constructions . . . er . . . obstructions. Right."

Dubious Leaders

The list of "men in charge" is a long one. The chances for humor are many when you deal with the pompous and the overambitious. There are a number of bosses, employers, who will always fill the bill by the nature of their given responsibilities. Ayckbourn seems to be suggesting that those in control of others have to walk a finer line than we mortals between respect and disrespect. And, of course, it is often obvious that in one play or another the playwright is resting easily in an assumed generality about bosses. There is also the sly difference between granted power and self-assuming power—together with the degree it is used. Graham *(Time and Time Again) does* employ people, but his chief failure is in the smallness of his vision, and his sniggering sexuality. He sees nothing redeeming whatsoever in Leonard's poetic ineptness. Harassing his brother-in-law is his life's pleasure. Another kind of pleasure, usually unfulfilled, are his attempts to give hands-on assistance to his attractive employee, Joan.

In the portraits of the up-and-coming Sid *(Absurd Person Singular)* and the back-sliding Sven *(Joking Apart)* we have the amusement of presiding over the gradual rise of one and descent of the other. Both plays cover a significant period of time and, therefore, have deliberate, realistic concerns. Ayckbourn means us to draw significance from the two accounts as well as the obvious humor. We watch the evolution in the character of Sid, from the first and second acts in which he is the laughable superhandyman, to the final act, in which he becomes the sadistic ring master of his friends, now turned helpless dancing charges.

Sven, on the other hand, presents an amusing history (over the twelve years of the play) of the evaporation of real power in his partnership with our hero, Richard. In Sven's continuing declarations of loss, we have some very clever lines. Unlike Sid, Sven is "given" attempts to analyze what is going on: "The fact is, when it comes down to it, you [Richard] have the one advantage over me that matters. You have flair, Richard. That's something that can't be learnt. It's handed out at birth, along with those other unfair advantages like physical beauty, under a most monstrously devised random system. And as always happens in these cases, it's always given to the very people who in my opinion do least to earn it. It's taken me forty-two years to think of that and I'm very depressed."

Any assessment of Ayckbourn must certainly give some attention to the accomplishment of twenty-eight plays over a fifteen-year period (1967–82). And at the age of forty-five there is the very real probability that before he is through he will have to be considered a major force in late twentieth-century drama. Of course, there is always a familiar problem when the reputations of authors such as Ayckbourn are seriously on the line. The fact of great commercial success always bothers academics and critics. Ironically, the same was a condition of Noel Coward's reputation, a playwright with whom Ayckbourn is often compared as a kind of Coward of the middle classes. However, as admirers such as Michael Billington (the *Guardian*) and Benedict Nightingale (the *New Statesman*) have repeatedly pointed out, this particular funny man has many funny and significant things to say. The agreement seems to be that he is a formidable entertainer—well trained with his Scarborough "company theater"—who has a remarkable insight into our present lives.

There is also a reverse effect involved that stems from his reputation as a comic writer. "Critics in all media often feel the need," Billington once pointed out, "to justify their calling by investing the ephemeral with cosmic significance."[7] That is not entirely the case here, as Billington argues, since there is *real* substance in Ayckbourn that needs no apology nor exaggerated esteem. And it should be further added that the reputation of being a good comic entertainer is one that needs no hiding behind. The creation of good, effective stage comedy has always been acknowledged as one of the most difficult tasks in writing. The persistent dilemma exists because the puritan in us laughs *but* always wonders why. "If a play does anything," Kenneth Tynan says, "either satirically or seriously, or tragically or farcically, to explain to me why I'm alive, it's a good play."[8]

Notes and References

Preface

    1. John Heilpern, "Striking Sparks off Suburbia," *Observer,* 13 February, 1977, 7.

    2. Benedict Nightingale, "Ayckbourn—Comic Laureate of Britain's Middle Class," *New York Times,* 25 March 1979, 4.

Chapter One

    1. Joan Buck, "Interview: Alan Ayckbourn," *Plays and Players,* September 1972, 29.

    2. Benedict Nightingale, "Ayckbourn—Comic Laureate of Britain's Middle Class," *New York Times,* 25 March 1979), 4.

    3. Robin Stringer, "Scarborough Fare," *Sunday Telegraph,* 5 April 1974, 30.

    4. Ian Watson, *Conversations with Ayckbourn* (London, 1981), 26.

    5. Ibid.

    6. Ibid., 27.

    7. Brian Connell, "A *Times* Profile Interview," *London Times,* 5 May 1976.

    8. Tom Sutcliffe, "The Ayckbourn Conquests," *Vogue,* 15 April 1975, 117.

    9. Connell, "A *Times* Profile Interview."

    10. Watson, *Conversations,* 37.

    11. Ibid., 37–38.

    12. Connell, "A *Times* Profile Interview."

    13. Peter Dacre, "Interview," *Sunday Express,* 14 September 1975, 11.

    14. John Russell Taylor, *The Second Wave: British Drama for the Seventies* (New York, 1971), 157.

    15. J. W. Lambert, *Drama,* Winter 1964, 24.

    16. Stringer, "Scarborough Fare," 32.

    17. Michael Coveney, "Scarborough Fare: An Interview with Alan Ayckbourn," *Plays and Players,* September 1975, 18.

    18. The other play, *The Story So Far,* opened in August 1970, had a number of title changes, but never reached London.

    19. Ronald Hayman, *London Times,* 7 April 1973.

    20. Ibid.

    21. Peter Lewis, *Daily Mail,* 17 August 1972.

    22. Coveney, "Scarborough Fare," 19.

    23. Ibid., 16.

24. Eric Shorter, *Sunday Telegraph*, 8 March 1979.
25. John Barber, *Daily Telegraph*, 15 October 1980.
26. Coveney, "Scarborough Fare," 19.
27. Anthony Curtis, *Financial Times*, 14 October 1981.
28. Stringer, "Scarborough Fare," 27.
29. Connell, "A *Times* Profile Interview."
30. Ibid.
31. Watson, *Conversations*, 87–88.
32. Ibid., 143.

Chapter Two

1. Ian Watson, "Ayckbourn of Scarborough," *Municipal Entertainment*, May 1978, 12.
2. Ibid. This play was the last to use the pen name, "Roland Allen."
3. *Mr. Whatnot* opened at the Arts Theatre on 6 August 1964 for a run of four weeks, starring Ronnie Barker.
4. Eric Rhode, *Plays and Players*, October 1964, 41.
5. Ibid.
6. *The Story So Far* was originally titled *Family Circles* and later *Me Times Me Times Me*.
7. Watson, "Ayckbourn of Scarborough," 14.
8. Ibid.

Chapter Three

1. *Jeeves* opened at Her Majesty's Theatre, London, 22 April 1975 for a run of one month. Books and lyrics were by Ayckbourn, music by Andrew Lloyd Webber. The cast included David Hemmings as Bertie Wooster, Michael Aldridge as Jeeves, Gordon Clyde as Harold "Stinker" Pinker, Christopher Good as Gussie Fink-Nottle, Bill Wallis as Sir Watkyn Bassett, John Turner as Sir Roderick Spode, Angela Easterling as Honoria Glossop, Gabrielle Drake as Madeline Bassett, Debbie Bowen as Stiffy Byng, and David Wood as Bingo Little. It was directed by Eric Thompson.
2. Coveney, "Scarborough Fare," 19.
3. Robin Stringer, "Scarborough Fare," *Sunday Telegraph*, 5 April 1974, 27.
4. Coveney, "Scarborough Fare" 19.
5. Ronald Bryden, *Plays and Players*, July 1975, 28.
6. Irving Wardle, *London Times*, 23 April 1975; Harold Hobson was another supporter.
7. Bryden, *Plays and Players*, 28.
8. *Surburban Strains*, a musical play by Ayckbourn and Paul Todd, (Scarborough, 1980), opened at the Round House Theatre, London for a

limited run—5 February 1981 to 14 March 1981, five weeks. The cast was essentially the original Scarborough Company: Lavinia Bertram as Carolyn, Robin Bowerman as Kevin, Robin Herford as Matthew; Allison Skilbeck (and others) played a number of roles. It was directed by Alan Ayckbourn.

9. *Men on Women on Men* was also a BBC television production in 1979.

10. Irving Wardle, *London Times,* 19 January 1980.

11. Ibid.

12. Anonymous, *Observer,* 27 January 1980.

13. Ibid.

14. Paul Allen, *New Statesman,* 25 January 1980, 142.

15. Watson, *Conversations,* 133.

16. Ibid., p. 134.

17. Ibid.

Chapter Four

1. *Relatively Speaking* (Scarborough, 1965, as *Meet My Father*) opened at the Duke of York's Theatre, London, on 29 March 1967, for one year. The cast included Richard Brier as Greg, Jennifer Hilary as Ginny, Michael Hordern as Philip, and Celia Johnson as Sheila. It was directed by Nigel Patrick.

2. Irving Wardle, *London Times,* 30 March 1967.

3. J. W. Lambert, *Drama,* Summer 1967, 25.

4. Ronald Hayman, "Interview," *London Times,* 4 July 1973.

5. B. A. Young, *Financial Times,* 31 March 1967.

6. "Countdown," *Mixed Doubles,* opened at the Comedy Theatre, London, on 9 April 1969 for a run of three months. The cast included Nigel Stock and Vivien Merchant. It was directed by Alex Dore. The other writers in the anthology of one-acters included John Bowen, Lyndon Brook, David Campton, George Melly, Alun Owen, Harold Pinter, James Saunders, and Fay Welden. Under the title, *We Who are about to. . . ,* the production first opened at the Hampstead Theatre Club on 6 February 1969.

7. *How The Other Half Loves* opened at the Lyric Theatre, London, for a run of two years. The cast included Robert Morley as Frank, Joan Tetzel as Fiona, Donald Burton as Bob, Heather Sears as Teresa, Brian Miller as William, and Elizabeth Ashton as Mary. It was directed by Robin Midgley. The play opened at the Royale Theatre, New York, on 29 March 1971 for three months. The cast included Phil Silvers as Frank, Bernice Massi as Fiona, Sandy Dennis as Teresa, Tom Aldredge as William, and Jeanne Heple as Mary. It was directed by George Saks. In the New York production William and Mary Featherstone are called Detweiler.

8. Irving Wardle, *London Times,* 6 August 1970, 6.

9. Clive Barnes, *New York Times,* 30 March 1971, 23.

10. Walter Kerr, *New York Times,* 4 April 1971, 3.
11. Watson, *Conversations,* 76.
12. Ibid., 77.
13. Ibid., 78.

Chapter Five

1. *Time and Time Again* (Scarborough, 1971) opened at the Comedy Theatre London, on 16 August 1972 for seven months. The cast included Michael Robbins as Graham, Bridget Turner as Anna, Tom Courtenay as Leonard, Cheryl Kennedy as Joan, and Barry Andrews as Peter. It was directed by Eric Thompson.
2. J. W. Lambert, *Drama,* Winter 1972, 15.
3. Ibid., 15.
4. Felix Barker, *Evening News,* 17 August 1972.
5. Charles Lewsen, *London Times,* 17 August 1972.
6. Frank Marcus, *Sunday Telegraph,* 20 August 1972.
7. Peter Lewis, *Daily Mail,* 17 August 1972.
8. John Russell Taylor, *Plays and Players,* October 1972, 40.
9. Brian Connell, "A Times Profile Interview," *London Times,* 5 May 1976.
10. *Absurd Person Singular* (Scarborough, 1972) opened at the Criterion Theatre, London, on 4 July 1973 and transferred to the Vaudeville Theatre for a total run of two years, four months (with *Bedroom Farce,* the two longest runs). The cast included Richard Brier as Sid, Bridget Turner as Jane, Michael Aldridge as Ronald, Sheila Hancock as Marion, David Burke as Geoffrey, and Anna Calder-Marshall as Eva. It was directed by Eric Thompson. The play opened at the Music Box Theatre, New York, in October 1974 for two years. The cast included Larry Blyden as Sid, Carole Shelley as Jane, Richard Kiley as Ronald, Geraldine Page as Marion, Tony Roberts as Geoffrey, and Sandy Dennis as Eva. It had the same director. The play won the *London Evening Standard* Drama Award for Best New Comedy of 1973. In November 1976 the play became Broadway's longest running current production, and the street sign at Broadway and 45th Street was changed to "Ayckbourn Alley."
11. John Barber, *Daily Telegraph,* 5 July 1973.
12. Preface to *Three Plays by Alan Ayckbourn* (New York, 1977), 7.
13. Robert Cushman, *Observer,* 8 July 1973.
14. Milton Schulman, *Evening Standard,* 5 July 1973.
15. Michael Billington, *Manchester Guardian,* 5 July 1973.
16. Robert Cushman, *Observer,* 8 July 1973.
17. Coveney, "Scarborough Fare," 19.
18. Janet Watts, *Observer,* 4 March 1979.
19. Ibid.

Chapter Six

1. *The Norman Conquests* (Scarborough, 1973) opened at the Globe Theatre, London, on 1 August 1974 for a year and a half. The cast included Tom Courtenay as Norman, Michael Gambon as Tom, Penelope Keith as Sarah, Felicity Kendal as Annie, Mark Kingston as Reg, and Bridget Turner as Ruth. It was directed by Eric Thompson. The play opened at the Morosco Theatre, New York, on 6 December 1975 for six months. The cast included Richard Benjamin as Norman, Paula Prentiss as Annie, Don Murray as Tom, Estelle Parsons as Sarah, Barry Nelson as Reg, and Carole Shelley as Ruth. It was directed by Eric Thompson. Thames TV, London, presented an excellent version in October 1977, starring Tom Conti as Norman. The play won the *London Evening Standard* and *Plays and Players'* drama awards for Best Play of 1974. In 1974, Ayckbourn received the Playwright of the Year Award from the Variety Club of Great Britain.
2. Preface to *The Norman Conquests* (London, 1975), 10.
3. Ibid., 11.
4. Irving Wardle, *London Times,* 9 August 1974.
5. Bernard Davies, *Broadcast,* 31 October 1977.
6. Jack Tinker, *Daily Mail,* 2 August 1974.
7. J. W. Lambert, *London Times,* 9 June 1974.

Chapter Seven

1. *Absent Friends* (Scarborough, 1974) opened at The Garrick Theatre, London, on 23 July 1975 for nine months. The cast included Peter Bowles as Paul, Pat Heywood as Diana, Ray Brooks as John, Cheryl Kennedy as Evelyn, Richard Brier as Colin, and Phyllida Law as Marge. It was directed by Eric Thompson. The play opened at the Kennedy Center, Washington, D.C., in July 1977 for a short run. The cast included Eli Wallach as Colin and Anne Jackson as Diana.
2. Irving Wardle, *London Times,* 24 July 1975.
3. Anonymous, *London Times,* 27 July 1975.
4. Ibid.
5. Michael Billington, *Guardian,* 24 July 1975.
6. Brian Connell, "A Times Profile Interview," *London Times,* 5 May 1976.
7. Coveney, "Scarborough Fare," 16.
8. *Confusions* (Scarborough, 1974) opened at the Apollo Theatre, London, on 19 May 1976 for a run of eight months. The cast included Pauline Collins as Lucy, Paula, Polly, Milly, and Beryl; Sheila Gish as Rosemary, Bernice, Mrs. Pearce, and Doreen; John Alderton as Harry, Waiter, Gosforth, and Arthur: Derek Fowlds as Terry, Martin, Stewart, and Ernest; James Cossins as Waiter ("Drinking Companions"), Pearce, Vicar, and Charles. It was directed by Alan Strachan.

9. Herbert Kretzmer, *Daily Express*, 21 May 1976.
10. Michael Billington, *Guardian*, 20 May 1976.
11. Ibid.

Chapter Eight

1. *Bedroom Farce* (Scarborough, 1975) opened at the National Theatre, London, on 16 March 1977 and transferred to the Prince of Wales Theatre for a total run of two years, four months. The cast included Michael Gough as Ernest, Joan Hickson as Delia, Michael Kitchen as Nick, Polly Adams as Jan, Derek Newark as Malcolm, Susan Littler as Kate, Stephen Moore as Trevor, and Maria Atken as Susannah. It was co-directed by Alan Ayckbourn and Peter Hall. The play opened at the Brooks Atkinson Theatre, New York, on 29 March 1979 for eight months. The cast was the original except for Michael Stroud as Nick and Delia Lindsey as Susannah. It had the same directors.
2. Bernard Levin, *London Times*, 20 March 1977.
3. Robert Cushman, *Observer*, 20 March 1977.
4. Preface to *Three Plays*, 8.
5. Jack Kroll, *Newsweek*, 9 April 1979.
6. Anthony Curtis, *Drama*, Summer 1977, 54.
7. *Just Between Ourselves* (Scarborough, 1976) opened at the Queen's Theatre London, on 20 April 1977 for five months. The cast included Colin Blakely as Dennis, Rosemary Leach as Vera, Michael Gambon as Neil, Constance Chapman as Marjorie, and Stephanie Turner as Pam. It was directed by Alan Strachan. The play won the *London Evening Standard* award for Best Play of 1977.
8. Irving Wardle, *London Times*, 21 April 1977.
9. Michael Billington, *Guardian*, 21 April 1977.
10. Preface to *Joking Apart and Other Plays* (London, 1979), 7.
11. Ibid.
12. Janet Watts, "Absurd Persons, Plural and Suburban," *Observer*, 4 March 1979: this is an interview.
13. Ibid.
14. Billington, *Guardian*.

Chapter Nine

1. *Ten Times Table* (Scarborough, 1977) opened at the Globe Theatre, London, on 5 April 1978 for a year. The cast included Paul Eddington as Ray, Ben Whitrow as Donald, Diane Bull as Phillipa, Julia McKenzie as Helen, Stephanie Fayerman as Sophie, John Salthouse as Eric, Matvelok Gibbs as Audrey, Tenniel Evans as Lawrence, Christopher Goodwin as Tim, and Rob Stuart as Max Kirkov. It was directed by Alan Ayckbourn.

2. Francis King, *Sunday Telegraph*, 9 April 1978.
3. Ibid.
4. Irving Wardle, *London Times*, 7 April 1978.
5. Anthony Curtis, *Drama*, Summer 1978, 55.
6. Benedict Nightingale, *New Statesman*, 14 April 1978, 504.
7. *Joking Apart* (Scarborough, 1978) opened at the Globe Theatre, London, on 7 March 1979 for a run of four months. The cast included Alison Steadman as Anthea, Christopher Cazenove as Richard, Julian Fellowes as Hugh, Marcia Warner as Louise, Robert Austin as Sven, Jennifer Piercey as Olive, John Price as Brian, and Diane Bull as Melody, Mandy, Mo, and Debbie. It was directed by Alan Ayckbourn. The play shared the *Plays and Players* award for Best Comedy of 1979.
8. Michael Billington, *Guardian*, 8 March 1979.
9. Irving Wardle, *London Times*, 2 February 1978.
10. Robert Cushman, *Observer*, 11 March 1979.
11. Milton Schulman, *Evening Standard*, 8 March 1979.
12. Ian Stewart, *Country Life*, 29 March 1979.
13. Benedict Nightingale, *New Statesman*, 16 March 1979.

Chapter Ten

1. *Sisterly Feelings* (Scarborough, 1979) opened at the National Theatre, London, on 3 June 1979 for a run of eight months. The cast included Anna Carteret as Dorcas, Penelope Wilton as Abigail, Stephen Moore as Simon, Michael Gambon as Patrick, Simon Callow as Stafford, Michael Bryant as Len, Andrew Cruickshank as Ralph, Selena Cadell as Brenda, and Susan Williamson as Rita. It was co-directed by Alan Ayckbourn and Christopher Morahan.
2. Jeremy Treglown, *Times Literary Supplement* 13 June 1980.
3. Mel Gussow, *New York Times*, 10 August 1980.
4. Robert Cushman, *Observer*, 8 February 1979.
5. John Barber, *Daily Telegraph*, 5 June 1980.
6. Treglown, *Times Literary Supplement*.
7. John Peter, *London Times*, 8 June 1980.
8. Anonymous, *Evening Standard*, 3 September 1980. Ben Travers (1886–1980) was widely known for his Aldwych Theatre farces in the 1920s and 1930s. In 1975, his first new play in twenty-three years, *The Bed Before Yesterday* was produced at the Lyric Theatre. The National Theatre revived *Plunder* (1928) in 1976.
9. *Taking Steps* (Scarborough, 1979) opened at the Lyric Theatre, London, on 2 September 1980 for nine months. The cast included Nicola Pagett as Elizabeth, Dinsdale Landen as Roland, Paul Chapman as Mark, Wendy Murray as Kitty, Michael Maloney as Tristram, and Richard Kane as Leslie. It was directed by Michael Rudman.

10. Sheridan Morley, "Steps in Time," *Punch*, 10 September 1980.

11. Irving Wardle, *London Times*, 3 September 1980.

12. Milton Shulman, "Knocking 'em for Six," *Evening Standard*, 3 September 1980.

13. Ibid.

Chapter Eleven

1. *Season's Greetings* (Scarborough, 1980) opened at the Round House Theatre London, for a limited run—14–25 October 1980. The cast was the original Scarborough Company: Michael Simkins as Neville, Tessa Peake-Jones as Belinda, Susan Vebel as Phyllis, Robin Herford as Harvey, Jeffrey Robert as Eddie, Lavinia Bertram as Pattie, Robin Bauerman as Clive, Ronald Herdman as Bernard, and Marcia Warren as Rachel. Opened at the Apollo Theatre, London on 29 March 1982. It was directed by Alan Ayckbourn.

2. Anonymous, *Scarborough Evening News*, 26 September 1980.

3. Linda Talbot, *Hampstead and Highgate Express*, 17 October 1980.

4. *Scarborough Evening News*, 26 September 1980.

5. Watson, *Conversations, 169–70.*

6. *Way Upstream* (Scarborough, 1981) opened at the Alley Theatre, Houston, on 24 February 1982, the American premiere, for a limited run of five weeks. Opened at the National Theatre, London on 18 August 1982. It was directed by Alan Ayckbourn.

7. Robin Thornber, *Guardian*, 5 October 1981.

8. Anthony Curtis, *Financial Times*, 14 October 1981.

9. Ibid.

10. Hermione Lee, *Times Literary Supplement*, 23 October 1981.

11. Desmond Pratt, *Yorkshire Post*, 5 October 1981.

12. Gerald Clarke, *Time*, 8 March 1982, 86.

13. Lee, *Times Literary Supplement.*

Chapter Twelve

1. Brian Connell, "A Times Profile Interview," *London Times*, 5 May 1976.

2. The father of modern farce is usually said to be Georges Feydeau (1862–1921)—especially his *L'Hôtel du Libre-Echange* (1894) and *La Dame de chez Maxim's* (1899). The best-known American farce is Brandon Thomas's *Charley's Aunt* (1892). The most recent farceur in Britain is the late Ben Travers (1886–1980).

3. Preface to *Joking Apart*, 8.

4. Ibid. 8–9.

5. Guido Almansi, "Victims of Circumstance: Alan Ayckbourn's Plays," *Encounter,* April 1978, 62.

6. Ibid, 64.

7. Michael Billington, *Guardian,* 14 August 1974.

8. Kenneth Tynan, cited by David Benedictus in a review of David Mercer's *Belcher's Luck, Plays and Players,* January 1967.

Selected Bibliography

PRIMARY SOURCES

1. Plays (first London production in parentheses)

Confusions: Five Interlinked One-Act Plays (1976). London: Samuel French, 1977.

Ernie's Incredible Illucinations (1971). London: Samuel French, n.d.

How the Other Half Loves (1970). London: Evans Plays, n.d.

Joking Apart and Other Plays: Just Between Ourselves and Ten Times Table (1979, 1977, 1978). London: Chatto & Windus, 1979.

Just Between Ourselves (1977). London: Samuel French, n.d.

Mixed Doubles (1969). London: Samuel French, n.d. Includes "Countdown.

Mr. Whatnot (1963). London: Samuel French, n.d.

The Norman Conquests (1974). London: Chatto & Windus, 1975; paperback reprint, London: Penguin Books, 1977.

Relatively Speaking (1967). London: Evans Plays, 1968.

Season's Greetings (1980). London: Samuel French, n.d.

Sisterly Feelings and Taking Steps (1980). London: Chatto & Windus, 1980.

Suburban Strains (1980). London: Samuel French, n.d.

Three Plays: Absurd Person Singular, Absent Friends and Bedroom Farce (1973, 1975, 1977). London: Chatto & Windus, 1977; paperback reprint, New York: Grove Press, 1977.

Time and Time Again (1972). London: Samuel French, n.d.

2. Essays and Interviews (a chronological listing)

Introduction to *Relatively Speaking*. London: Evans Plays, 1968.

"Provincial Playwriting." *Author*, Spring 1970, 25.

"A Farceur, Relatively Speaking." *Guardian*, 7 August 1970, 8. Interview by Robin Thornber.

Interview by Joan Buck. *Plays and Players*, September 1972, 29.

Interview by Ronald Hayman. *London Times*, 4 July 1973.

Preface to *The Norman Conquests*. London: Chatto & Windus, 1975.

"Scarborough Fare." *Plays and Players*, September 1975, 18. Interview by Michael Coveney.

Interview by Peter Dacre. *Sunday Express*, 14 September 1975.

"A Times Profile Interview". *London Times*, 5 May 1976. Interview by Brian Connell.

Preface to *Three Plays*. New York: Grove Press, 1977.

"Striking Sparks off Suburbia." *Observer*, 13 February 1977. Interview by John Heilpern.

Preface to *Joking Apart and Other Plays*. London: Chatto & Windus, 1979.

"A Playwright on the Prom". *Sunday Telegraph*, 28 January 1979, 9. Interview by Rosemary Say.

"Absurd Persons, Plural and Suburban." *Observer*, 4 March 1979. Interview by Janet Watts.

SECONDARY SOURCES

Almansi, Guido. "Victims of Circumstances: Alan Ayckbourn's Plays." *Encounter*, April 1978, 58–65. An excellent analysis of the plays, demonstrating essential values and importance.

Clarke, Gerald. "This Realm, This Little England." *Time*, 8 March 1982. Review of the latest play, *Way Upstream*, in its American premiere in Houston, Texas.

Elsom, John. *Post War British Theatre*. London: Routledge & Kegan Paul, 1976. A valuable summary of contemporary dramatists and their work.

Hayman, Ronald. *British Theatre Scene Since 1955*. London: Oxford University Press, 1979. Good appraisals by *London Times* critic.

————. *London Times*, 7 April 1973. Surveys Ayckbourn's early plays.

Joseph, Stephen. *Theatre in the Round*. London: Barrie and Rockliff, 1967. Good account by the founder of the Scarborough Theatre, and Ayckbourn's mentor.

Kalem, T. E. "Manic High." *Time*, 9 April 1979, 76–78. Review of New York production of *Bedroom Farce*. Surveys major plays and career. Good biographical material.

Kerensky, Oleg. *The New British Drama: Fourteen Playwrights since Osborn and Pinter*. London: Hamish Hamilton, 1977. A major account of the plays and career—"farce came to me naturally."

Nightingale, Benedict. "Ayckbourn—Comic Laureate of Britain's Middle Class." *New York Times*, 25 March 1979. On the occasion of *Bedroom Farce* in New York, a first-page feature article. Valuable insights into the career. Good personal portraits.

Stringer, Robin. "Scarborough Fare." *Sunday Telegraph*, 5 April 1974, 27–32. A revealing personal interview which shows the development of present dramatic traits.

Sutcliffe, Tom. "The Ayckbourn Conquests." *Vogue*, 15 April 1975, 117. Basic biographical information. Appraises his technique.

Taylor, John Russell. *The Angry Theatre: New British Drama*. New York: Hill & Wang, 1969. Reliable commentary by a major critic, with history of the early Scarborough theater.

————. *The Second Wave: British Drama for the Seventies*. New York: Hill & Wang, 1971. Perceptive appraisals of recent theater.

Watson, Ian. "Ayckbourn of Scarborough." *Municipal Entertainment*, May 1978, 7–17. The most complete account of the plays, major and minor. Illustrations of Scarborough and London productions.

————. *Conversations with Ayckbourn*. London: Macdonald Futura, 1981. Valuable "extended interview" with former theatrical associate.

Index